Nectar of Nondual Truth

No. 38

CONTENTS

10 God As Mother
by Swami Aseshananda
Seeing God as Mother is not just for the sake of changing the gender of God, though that may be long overdue, but more that She is supremely independent in Her own right. She is our very power at all levels. The many realms of existence fall under Her auspice and purview.

15 The Dire Effects Of Vismriti
by Babaji Bob Kindler
A mind may be a terrible thing to waste, but losing a retentive memory is a calamitous misfortune. Loss of the precious memories and knowledge gleaned in past life times only returns to us in this present one, leaving us to do it all over again until finally our freedom is won.

21 Vedanta 101 - Teachings On Peace
by the SRV Staff
Overcoming brooding mind via thinking mind resulting in illumined mind is the precious instruction serious practitioners of dharma and jnanam find in the comprehensive path of Vedanta.

23 Blossoming Of Consciousness
by Swami Brahmeshananda
The appearance of the loving Lord in human form, Sri Ramakrishna, has taken this world by shocked surprise. One facet of His advent is the great privilege of watching Him express His full-blown divinity, from shanti to samadhi, in front of the wondering and adoring eyes of millions of living beings.

29 Is Our Practice Bringing Transformation?
by Anam Thubten
If spiritual self-effort fails to work for the practitioner of today, then the accompanying practice of adjusting the mind's habit patterns and utilizing the supremely natural way of simple opening to transparent awareness is advised.

37 Religious Views As Foundational
by Prof. Larry A. Herzberg
Transforming skepticism into sharing, criticism into contribution, argumentation into articulation, opinion into opportunity, is accomplished by adopting the simple perspective of accepting the basic teachings of all religious traditions at the level of sincerity that they require and deserve.

39 Godblogs And Brahman Bytes
by Babaji Bob Kindler
More nectar nuggets from the rich goldmine of Sri Ramakrishna's radiant mind, are offered once again for contemplation.

41 Seeing The Face Of God
by Rabbi Rami Shapiro
The healing and transformative practice of *Shiviti*, or seeing God in the faces of others, as well as striving to free the narrow mind from its prison resulting in the attainment of expansive mind, form the key teachings in this enlightening article.

43 Interview With Pir Vilayet Khan
by Alexander Hixon
Centering around the most current message of our times according to contemporary Sufism, the engaging dialogue in this interview places the pros and cons of conventional religious observances side by side with the ardent pursuit and attainment of rare mysticism.

48 Absolute Reality & God
by Annapurna Sarada
Bringing more clarity to the meaning of the word God, and further delineating the need for specifying the difference between God with form and beyond form, outlines the emphasis of this article based in deep Vedantic thought.

"Would to God that all souls following and worshipping along all of these many wisdom pathways could live together as free and easily in the world as their religions do in this honorable journal."

Publisher's Page

Sarada Ramakrishna Vivekananda – SRV Associations
"Setting the feet of humanity on the path of Universal Truth."

Notes on an Advaitic Journal

At the basis of Advaita as the philosophy of Shankara and his gurus, there is Advaita as experience. Advaita as experience represents that supreme place where all diversity merges in its Essence. It is not combatant or immiscible with qualified or dualistic approaches, but rather provides them their place of consummate arrival. Where actual practice rather than mere book learning is emphasized, where religion, philosophy and spirituality are not separate from one another, where knowledge and love, reason and devotion, are never divorced from each other, there does the truth of authentic nonduality effloresce.

Historically speaking, experiential Advaita originated with the ancient Rishis. Therefore, the Upanisads contain the nondual truths of the Vedas which declare: idam mahabhutam anantam aparam vijnanaghana eva, "This great Being is endless and without limit. It is a mass of indivisible Consciousness only."

SRV Associations & Universality

The SRV Associations are part of a worldwide movement of spiritual aspirants devoted to the study and practice of Vedanta and Divine Mother Wisdom. The ideals of this ancient pathway to God, exemplified in the lives of Sri Sarada Devi, Sri Ramakrishna and Swami Vivekananda, are the original and eternal perfection of the Soul and its inherent oneness with Reality, the manifesting of divinity in our lives, selfless service of all beings as God, and reverence for the ultimate unity of all sacred traditions. To this end our purpose is to study, worship, and contemplate Truth so that spirituality may flourish. This is the Advaitic way — "None else but Self, none other than Mother."

Nectar's Mission — Advaita-Satya-Amritam

In Sanskrit, amrita, nectar also means Immortality – and this is, indeed, what we are offering: opportunities to become aware of this Amrita that is our very Essence via the rarefied teachings from Vedanta and the World Religions and Philosophies that appear in each issue of Nectar.

Nectar of Non-Dual Truth is SRV Associations' heartfelt offering of highest Wisdom to the human community. It is the sincerest form of love and service we know to disseminate non-dual Truth and teachings which transmit pure knowledge, pure love, and true universality. Through Nectar we are working out SRV's mission of spiritual upliftment and education. Please join us; this is a universal movement.

Keeping Nectar in Print
Subscribe to Nectar of Non-Dual Truth

Nectar of Nondual Truth, or *Advaitasatyamrita* in Sanskrit, is a subscription-based instrument of Universal Religious & Philosophical Teachings. It requires subscriptions to stay in print. Please subscribe to Nectar using the form at the back of this issue.

You Can Help Others Receive Nectar

We continue to supply free copies to prison inmates, religious organizations, and low income persons in the U.S. You can help bridge the financial gap with a separate donation to Nectar. SRV Associations is a 501(c)3 tax-exempt organization.

To donate online, Visit: www.srv.org > Giving. To donate by check, mail to: SRV Associations, PO Box 1364, Honokaa, HI 96727 (payable to: SRV Associations)

808-990-3354 | srvinfo@srv.org | www.srv.org

With reverent gratitude, we heartily thank the contributing writers of this issue of Nectar of Nondual Truth, who have so graciously and selflessly shared the wisdom of their respective traditions and practices.

Staff of Nectar of Nondual Truth

Publisher
Sarada Ramakrishna Vivekananda Associations
* an Annual Publication

For more information concerning the SRV Associations or Nectar of Nondual Truth please contact:
SRV Associations, PO Box 1364, Honoka'a, HI 96727
Phone: (808) 990-3354
e-mail: srvinfo@srv.org   website: www.srv.org
Nectar Subscription is on a donation basis only

No part of this publication may be reproduced or transmitted in any form without permission from the publisher. Entire contents copyright 2023. All Rights Reserved. ISSN 1531-1414

Editor
Babaji Bob Kindler

Associate Editor
Annapurna Sarada

Production
Lokelani Kindler

Cover Image:
Photo by Babaji

Acknowledgement
Image of Ramakrishna's Disciples
Courtesy of Vedanta Press
800-816-2242

Contributing Writers
Swami Aseshananda
Swami Brahmeshananda
Anam Tulku Thubten
Rabbi Rami Shapiro
Prof. Larry Herzberg
Annapurna Sarada
Alexander Hixon
Babaji Bob Kindler

EDITORIAL

Within the profound pages of Nectar of Nondual Truth *are to be found the teachings and perspectives of various adherents of the major religions of the world, all expressing different aspects of the one Eternal Religion. It strives to be in line with Swami Vivekananda's vision, expressed by him, in part, as:* "Mankind ought to be taught that religions are but the varied expressions of The Religion which is Oneness, so that each may choose the path that suits him best." *He followed this by saying,* "Create a school to teach comparative religions. Teach Sanskrit, the different schools of Vedanta and some European languages. Have a press and papers printed in vernacular. When all that is done I will know that you have accomplished something. If you could start a magazine on Vedantic lines it would further our object. Be positive; do not criticize others. Be always ready to concede to the opinions of your brethren, and try always to conciliate."

Now in its 23rd year, and on its 38th issue, Nectar continues to present philosophical flowers from the fragrant bouquet of Universality to all and sundry, after first lovingly offering them at the Holy Feet of the Wisdom Mother of the Universe by Her illumined sons and daughters. This is so because there must be a few places on this beleaguered earth where both religious harmony and nondual Truth are held up as supreme ideals which all and everyone can strive for. This is further so because mankind, stripped of its misdirections and misconceptions, is God, and the practice and attainment of the harmony of all religious traditions is the way to this singular and superlative realization.

Therefore, when the Rig Veda states, "Ekam sat vipra bahudda vadanti," *that* "Truth is One, but there are many paths leading to it;" *or when it declares,* "God is One, but seers call It by different names," *this is ample reason to rejoice and celebrate both the One and the Many. Certainly, there is no cause for disagreement and argument in this, what to speak of warring between beings from different religions, or even among the adherents of the same religion!*

And so, this issue of Nectar holds teachings of Truth from sacred traditions such as Judaism, Sufism, Vedanta, Tibetan Buddhism, with elements of Shaktism and Western Philosophy as well, as naturally as an orchard contains luscious fruits of varying types. In the past it has presented wisdom from Zen Buddhism, Taoism, Christianity, Jainism, with flavoring from adherents of the religion of the Quakers, of Shamanism, Western Psychology and more. Would to God that all souls following and worshipping along all of these many wisdom pathways could live together as free and easily in the world as their religions do in this honorable journal.

The powerful presence of Sri Ramakrishna is to be found throughout the pages of this journal, who besides being considered the Avatar of this present age by so many, is also the foremost representative of the doctrine of the harmony of all religions. In Him, Universality gets perfectly married to the principle of nonduality (advaita). He, the Holy Mother, and Their divine sons and daughters are thus busy helping living beings cast off the weights of unhealthy compromise and mundane convention by taking up the banner of peace, love, and light. This amounts, in part, to the welcome return of beneficial good will residing in the hearts of living beings.

"That nameless, formless, unseen Essence,
Whom the realized seers call by many inspiring names, such as,
The Divine Atmosphere, the Waters of Life, the Fire of Yoga,
The Open Sky of Awareness, the Carrier of Consciousness.
The Devourer of Death, and the One who shines forth the Light,
Is also the Eternal Companion dwelling within all beings."

Om Peace, Peace, Peace

Babaji Bob Kindler

NECTAR OF ADVAITIC INSTRUCTION

Questions from Our Readers

When sincere devotees discover what profundity lies at the depths of both Indian philosophy, as well as in their own minds, they formulate effective questions designed to bring such revelations and insights up to the surface of everyday awareness so that all beings can either deepen their practice or generate interest in the dharma.

"When one becomes enlightened – as in that final enlightenment (although I'm not even certain what full enlightenment is) – can one come back to this world should they desire to?"

When fully enlightened beings merge their body/mind mechanisms into nondual Reality, i.e., into Brahman, they enter Mahasamadhi, not just samadhi. It is much like the Buddha, who reached Mahanirvana, not just nirvana. These distinctions in both the lives of luminaries and in the Sanskrit language itself shed light on such matters.

However, a more definitive answer comes when we consider Sri Ramakrishna and His 16 direct disciples, all of whom lived in recent times. The Great Master told us that some certain souls can gather their minds back from total immersion. The greater percentage of practitioners and adepts cannot manage this, nor can the "ordinary" saints, sages, and seers. Only souls who are Ishvarakotis, those who attend upon Avatars when they come to earth and embody, are able to retrieve Consciousness back to form after it has merged into formless Awareness.

This makes more sense when we observe how He went into nondual samadhi and came out many times in His later life. Sometimes it took Him a little while to become fully aware of His surroundings and the devotees in His room after being in formless Awareness. He had difficulty recognizing His own wife, the Holy Mother, as well as His precious Naren (Swami Vivekananda), while in that state – the point being that the same thing occurs when one dissolves completely, never to return again, but somehow is able to do so by His own vested powers.

This gets reiterated when a fully illumined soul returns after death to take another body, or incarnation. They begin to remember people, places, teachings, etc., from their past lifetimes, as the haze of being beyond form, possibly for hundreds of years, begins to thin and dissipate.

In conclusion, and for clarification, highly attained souls can come back to embodiment on earth, but they do it consciously, and by their own inherent powers. Millions of other souls come back as well, but they are dragged back by "desire," as you wrote, inadvertently, above, in your question. They only remember how to forage for food, seek pleasures and an earthly/worldly living – like "*the birds and the beasts of the field.*" But "*birds have nests, and foxes have holes,*" meaning that the human being, who is not essentially an animal, is not of earth, but of Formless Awareness.

"I've been doing pranayam practice now for almost nine years, yet I don't experience any of the inner sounds I used to hear. What might be the significance of this? Also, I can't seem to go any further than the 6-24-12 count as it seems I just don't have the lung capacity."

To try and put this gently, both those sounds you heard early on in your practice, and also pranayama itself, are beginning signs of spiritual awakening. Students should be taught (if they will but take learned gurus) that such phenomena and efforts are like signposts that point the way; one does not have to pick up a signpost and carry it home, but should leave it where it is for others to see.

A man once dove into a deep lake and swam to the bottom. While down there he did not breath. When he surfaced he took breaths again. When the fourth limb of Yoga, called pranayam, has been mastered, it becomes like a trusty old tool that the mechanic leaves in his toolchest, only taking it out for certain tasks. Like this, exercise and breathing practice are to be put aside when it comes time for climbing to higher limbs. When inbreath, held breath, and outbreath become equal, the practice phase is over. Then, as the Upanisads say, natural kumbhaka occurs – which really means that one does not breathe anymore, i.e., never again breathes the air of worldliness, but breathes only in Brahman.

At that sublime point, intended as a culmination free of backtracking, one does not have to say, "Oh my God, I did not do my pranayam practice today!" It is the same with the mantra, and with meditation, except these take longer to master. In the teachings, like the commentators on Patanjali's Yoga, a few months is all it will take for one to master pranayam. For some, it will not take even that long.

This tendency of Westerners to make asana and pranayam all of Yoga both draws out the practice phase unnecessarily, and places the goal always beyond reach, at a great distance. Asana and pranayam cannot give one Enlightenment anyway; all the great ones agree upon that. As one song of India sings, "*If merely breathing in and out could cause liberation, then even a bellows or a hot air balloon would be enlightened.*"

Move on up the tree of Yoga and begin to control the mind so it can concentrate and meditate free of body and lungs. Enlightenment only becomes more possible if one draws close to the higher limbs, and does not hang out on the lower ones. For those illumined ones, they use that purified mind to control prana, senses, and body. Use them as your example, and swiftly ascend the ladder of practice to duly arrive at the mountaintop of direct spiritual experience.

And why this preoccupation with counting breaths, and mantras as well? The Holy Mother has told us that to concentrate the mind on the Ideal – even for a few minutes – is far better than increasing lung capacity, counting how many mantras one has done each day, and meditating for hours devoid of any beneficial results. The Father of Yoga, himself, has given the instruction that to fully concentrate the mind for even seven seconds is a minor samadhi. Want a real challenge? Try that! Nine months with the lungs or seven seconds with formless Awareness, it is not a hard choice; it is a no-breather....

"RY Lesson #38 provided much clarity on the dynamics of how samskaras are maintained and how the kleshas reinforce and create new samskaras. I also greatly appreciate the delineation of how these samskaras and their effects are both gross and subtle and how one can and should leverage kriya-yoga to do away with the gross manifestations of the samskaras and viveka-dhyan to do away with their subtle manifestations (I know we have discussed this before, but repetition is proving to be the spice of spiritual life, as one Great Soul has imprinted on this mind). This understanding, along with the reinforcement of constant practice, has deepened my understanding of how to handle the various subtleties of the mind in meditation and in action. These lessons are simply amazing! How did you become so adept in Raja Yoga?"

The phase of constant practice that you mention above, combined with guidance from an illumined guru, and adherence to the swift path of Jnana Yoga, was my yogic route. I came into this life and body with love for God, or bhakti, already, so the ground was fertile for "growth." Along the way, I found Swami Vivekananda early on, who filled me in on *"the Atman that never grows,"* and *"never comes and goes"* either. Ironically, that nondual piece that destroys the idea of growth also swiftens growth. It destroys the incomplete idea of evolution by adding in involution. It destroys the false view of birth and death by proving the Soul to be unoriginated.

And to the point of your comments here, teachings from Mother India's Raja Yoga clarify the confused mind by revealing the contents of the mind for study, i.e., sankalpa and samskaras. To this revelation it adds tools with which one can regain real yogic powers, such as viveka-khyati, via pat methods such as Kriya Yoga. And so we continue to explore Raja Yoga again and again, since repetition is the spice of spiritual life.

"I may be skipping ahead a bit, but what constitutes the preferred form of Ishwara Pranidana? Is any divine being considered appropriate?"

Ishvara is a singular and exceptional Soul, a Soul of souls. Patanjali explains this in certain sutras the Raja Yoga study. But he also has a system that lists seven ways of mastering the mind, and meditating upon an illumined soul is one of them. Basically, the Avatars are from Ishvara, so seekers would focus on Them for Ishvara Pranidana. But then, who is an illumined soul worthy of selecting for meditation purposes? Again, people may disagree on that, preferring different deities. The discerning devotee should be able to see, by close scrutiny, who is worthy of veneration. Big egos, usage of occult powers, desire to dominate, greed for power and money, relying upon sensational spectacle, etc., these would betray many a candidate for the title of enlightenment. One has only to watch – even if it takes several decades – for the truth to emerge. But for Ishvara/Ishvari, they are fairly obvious. I have been mediating on that Rama and Krishna who is Sri Ramakrishna for over 50 years now. How grateful I am, with no regrets and many pranams.

"I'm facing a situation with my job and I'm at a crossroads about how to proceed. One devotee posted this quote which is highly relevant: 'Surrendering all actions to Me, with your thoughts resting on Self, freed from hope and selfishness and cured of mental fever, engage in battle.' (Gita 3.30). Swami Chidbhavananda comments: 'The more one attunes one's mind to truth, the more one gains in equilibrium. The truth is, the Lord is the invisible propeller of all actions in the universe. He is the true owner of everything sentient and insentient. Man's prerogative is to know this truth and adjust his life activities accordingly. His mental fever gets pacified in that way. Further, efficiency in the execution of duty increases in him.' Mental fever is a great way to describe how I feel at work each day. For me to be successful, it appears I would need to dedicate significant time to studying these work related items. I see no other way around it. Alternatively, I could seek a job which likely pays less, but is less demanding. I know you are a guru of spiritual matters, and not worldly matters, but in light of the quote above, what is the dharmic way of approaching this?"

In Vedanta, we certainly do emphasize spiritual life and its attainment, but the practical teachings Vedanta gives deal effectively with the area of earthly concerns as well. Thus, a question such as yours, here, appears in our nondual journal for clarification, along with and side by side with those of high philosophical content. For instance, the problem of mental fever is taken up by the swami quoted above, indicating that Gita, Krishna, swamis, and gurus are here to clear and balance matters.

It seems that no concern is too small to address, then, the only criterion being if the seeker deeply wants a resolution, if the seeker will listen and apply the solution to the problem, and mainly, if the concern is getting in the way of spiritual realization. To continue to live under the weight of said problem or problems, even after the solution has been given and seen, is a sign of weakness that is all too common in families and workplaces today. To brook no compromise, to accept no failure, is the decision of the wise. To quote the Gita gain, *"Many-branching are the decisions of the restless of mind, but single-branched is the way of the wise."*

So remain in the atmosphere of these teachings and implement them in your life, work, and mind. You will find that solutions come, balance returns, and a greater light attends upon all of life.

"I have been thinking of the tanmatras and working to mature my understanding of them. Originally I thought of them as a type of thought which is then manifested on this earth and in the mind (knowing that all this is in the mind). But it seems that what the scriptures point towards and what has dawned on the mind, is that they are the very substance which makes up thought and thought forms. I also see how these tanmatras are filled with Consciousness and Intelligence, though they are inert by themselves and through the power of Intelligence and Consciousness become concrete (as it were). It seems that through inspecting these tiny particles, tanmatras, one can enter into the Infinite…one just needs to 'split open' such wisdom particles. So previously, prior to your teachings, the mind thought that wisdom particles were a subset of thoughts, but now I see how all substances, made up of tanmatras, are wisdom particles. One simply needs to have the correct orientation. Is the above revelation rightly understood?"

As Swamiji has taught us, tanmatras are a finer state of matter. Out of them, all that the senses go by and depend upon are manufactured. Tanmatras, to senses, to objects, from the inner to the outer, this process returns to us the renewed wisdom of old India, forgotten in Western science, biology, and psychology. Now we only need to connect it all inwards to the mind, and beyond.

For more teachings consult the book, *Footfalls of the Indian Rishis*, wherein several deep charts and their teachings appear.

"I greatly appreciate how Lord Patanjali (as well as Swamiji and Vedavyasa) place the responsibility for purifying and controlling this mind in the hands of the student. During my meditations I have most certainly been taking this stance of applying self-effort to find subtle barriers and penetrate through them. Nevertheless, I find that there are times during meditation where I can't penetrate in order to progress further. During these times, the mind is starting to feel as if 'now it needs to be open to Mother's Grace,' and that my responsibility is to hold the mind in such a state as long as I can until Mother provides more insight into how to move forward. Is having these two modes of the mind beneficial and productive for progress?

Beneficial, yes, and even essential. The two wings of the bird, in this case one's own self-effort combined with the Grace of Divine Mother, or one's Ishtam, are an infallible way to not only "get off the ground," but also grow spiritually and reach the ultimate Goal. Even that potential problem of goal-orientation itself will be avoided by taking refuge in Her Grace and guidance. Just keep up the practice on your own, checking in with the gurus.

"My eyes generally rest lightly closed during both japa and formless meditation. Should I work on having my eyes gently open, looking down past the tip of the nose? If, so, is it more prescribed for the japa practice, formless meditation, or both?"

I would interpret looking down the tip of the nose as gazing into the heart. Care must be taken to avoid the sensationalism of the hatha yoga system, and its skewed permutations as it came West. For therein one finds the occult power version of things, i.e., the asana assumed for body alone as a longevity tactic, instead of the self-surrender of allowing Shakti/Divine Mother to take over the body for purification of all aspects of existence; also, the breathing for enjoying the flow of prana in the senses' contact with their objects, instead of balancing the breath, mastering it, then connecting it inwards to the psychic prana to purify mind and thoughts so as to gain Enlightenment.

These lower practices and their proponents would have one focusing attention actually on the nose so that one could enjoy aromas and enhance sensual experience. Looking past the nose, or down the bridge of the nose, with eyes half closed, infers that the eyes are not looking outward at all; why would a meditator want to do that? Is the nose an illumined soul? When meditation is purposefully done on the senses as alambanas, in that exercise, that is for transcending said senses after noting their place and purpose (to know the cosmic order of things/tattvas, out and in). Only bhogi-yogis cling out there so as to enjoy and smell all manner of aromas here and there. Pseudo-yogis who write autobiographies on themselves get fascinated with that type of thing. The serious seeker after Freedom focuses attention in the heart; that is what is meant by "gazing down the tip of the nose."

If one studies the famous meditation pose of Vivekananda one can see he is fully concentrated within, even with the eyes slightly open. In the case of hatha yogis, one sees them actually looking at the tip of the nose, with the eyes crossed; a silly expression on their faces, inciting laughter.

At the other end of the spectrum, pertinent to these skewed views, is the fellow who rolls the eyes up in to the head, with said focus on the third eye, or something. It is rather an all whites and no yolk affair, kind of scary, like an alien has come amongst us. These types leave the eyes open to show others how high and transcendental they have become, like a "watch me now as I go into nirvikalpa in an instant," type of blowhard's demonstration.

The Upanisads instruct to keep the concentration (inner gaze) focused in the heart center, anahata chakra, while the authentic Kundalini system advises that one is to let it rise to other centers in good time at the behest of Kundalini Shakti when She is ready to bestow such inner movement. By the time She reaches the Vishuddha chakra, eyes are closed permanently…no egg whites, no view of the outer throat, nor, of course, the eyes, ears, and nose, etc. Not only the outer senses, but also the inner senses are dissolving. If the lids happen to open, the eyes are pools of bliss — as in the samadhi picture of Sri Ramakrishna, which, as Holy Mother's direct disciple, Swami Nityaswarupananda, once told me, was the first time in history that God had ever been photographed.

So as you can tell by the range of my response on the eyes, it is more that the meditator's attention falls away from them rather than upon them — unless you are taking one up as a specific alambana in order to find out its connection to the others, especially for purposes of involution (leading to dissolution). As for the breathing processes themselves, Swamiji gives a few simple ones in the Raja Yoga book. He does not intend for the student to do them without instructions from and observation by a guru. Again, there are breathing practices in hatha yoga, there are the same concerning the more comprehensive Vedic breathing, and also rightly-oriented Tantric breathing exercises. The latter two are infinitely superior, while the first one risks disorientation and attachment to the body. When next we meet, we can deepen your practice and increase the power in them by increments, making sure not to overdo them or spend an inordinate amount of time on them, as there is much more to Yoga and its practice than body and breath.

"Swamiji describes a practice of Pranayama involving the Ida and Pingala, connected with breathing-in through alternate nostrils, and with certain patterns. I am also aware that this can be a dangerous/injurious practice if not done properly, with a teacher, and at the correct time for the aspirant. With my practice, I continue to balance the four parts of the inbreath, held breath, outbreath, and held again (aligning them with 'I am Brahman, I will always be Brahman, I am not the world.') Currently, I would say that I hold those breaths for roughly four to six seconds. I only do this practice briefly, after opening the shrine with the traditional SRV Arati. I have found that this breathing practice helps calm wayward thoughts, and allows me to concentrate more deeply and powerfully during japa and formless meditation. I will also do a dissolving of the mindstream practice before starting japa during some meditations (this is easier for me when I have had vivid dreams the night before, as I use the dream senses and dream elements to help in the dissolution process). Should I look to incorporate a more detailed and defined Pranayama? Or would you say that the practice of balancing of the four parts of the breath is enough of a breathing exercise for my current practice (to help aid in one-pointed concentration)?"

Along with what you are learning and have incorporated of the Vedic breathing practice, what you are doing to complement it is both safe and expansive of mind. We can work further to help you expand the lungs a bit so as to benefit from all of this more directly. What is not being brought forward here is the import of connecting the rounds of breathing more philosophically, like to one's states of consciousness, and The Word. Attending satsangs will help with that, including viewing specific SRV classes that take up such special teachings on Vedic breathing, and that are not found in today's yoga circles. Write in with more specific questions on this as they surface.

"I just finished afternoon meditation/contemplation, and what I wanted to concentrate the mind on was how to get past the intellectual frame of reference. This past seminar was simply great, and I came out of it wanting to squeeze more from all that I have studied and continue to study. In order to do this and dive deeper, I see a big step being getting beyond the intellectual frame of reference. When I was contemplating this topic and holding it in the mind, a few thoughts came forth from the depths. The first one was informing the mind that all knowledge comes from the Devi, and that what we call understanding is simply that knowledge that She chooses to share with us. The second thought that followed this was the letting go of ownership of knowledge. These two thoughts are tightly related, and I wanted to check with you in order to see if my mind was feeding me reliable information. Upon thinking of these two responses to my contemplation, the importance of maintaining concentration and controlling the speed of the mind (i.e. keep it operating intentionally) seem to be two essential practices (until they become fixed states of the mind) which will enable me to successfully allocate all knowledge to the rightful owner and relinquishing all sense of ownership over the 'learned knowledge.' For when the mind is not held tightly and still in its training phase, it seems that it is far too easy (especially with the English language) to adopt ownership when thinking and contemplating what 'one knows.' I would greatly appreciate your thoughts on this matter and if you have any further instructions for how I can further work towards going beyond the intellectual frame of reference."

The first thing that comes up when reading your very astute summation here, is the practice of making observations on the ego in this process. Both the mind and the intellect are under the control of the ego in this day and age. It is certainly true in today's intellectual arenas of the West, and the lack of this scrutinizing observation of the ego's co-opting of thought and intelligence for its own aims and ends is responsible for both misdirections and blockages along the trajectory of thought, actions, and their results. You have mentioned several of these here.

Briefly, when the heart and mind get together and collaborate with one another to assure that all the knowledge that dawns from the intellect's serious studies gets offered back to the Mother and not to the individual ego, then the orientation is corrected. Soon, no more arrogant skewing of ownership and agency will transpire. It may take a while in those who attempt it, but there will be no jivanmukti (spiritual freedom) or any jivanmuktas (unbound souls) in the West until it is accomplished.

For the serious seeker of Freedom, then, a deep look at the individual ego and the constant effort to dissolve it into Divine Reality — first into the Ishtam, then into Brahman — will comprise a major aspect of his or her sadhana.

"I have compared viveka-dhyan to Swamiji's commentary on Raja Yoga sutra II.10: 'When the Chitta, which is an effect, is resolved into its cause, Asmita or Egoism, then only will the fine impressions die along with it. Meditation cannot destroy these.' Can you help me understand the difference between the meditation that Swamiji is mentioning here, and the practice of viveka-dhyan when trying to rid the mind of its samskaras? I'm wondering if Swamiji is approaching getting rid of samskaras in the chitta from a level of having to attain Samadhi in order to truly return the samskaras to their cause (Asmita), and thus remove them from the mind?"

The meditation practice wherein meditators just sit daily and let the mind wander, will not purify the mind. Neither will that meditation that strives to attain emptiness get at the inhibiting causes he mentions here. The meditation of discrimination, which is consciously accompanied by discrimination, alone can do that. Focus of mind is much higher than emptiness of mind, unless what one means by the term "emptiness," ironically enough, is that mind empty of just those impeding things that viveka-dhyan effectively removes.

The great ones, whose egos got reduced, know that the mind collects impurities like a mirror collects dust. They continue to practice in order to keep it as clear as possible. One cannot pretend mental impurities away by surface meditation; nor, can one transcend those impurities and come back to the mind station later and expect them to be gone.

So, meditation without a focus is almost worthless; meditation with a focus but devoid of discrimination is better but unlikely to remove karmas and samskaras in the mind. It is focus with discrimination that clarifies the mind, i.e., khyati, and renders it able to take the practitioner to Brahman, or Ishvara if that is the aim. As Swamiji said, one cannot clean clothes with muddy water. Expecting the mind that merely meditates daily to accomplish the removal of age-old impressions from acts done in many previous lifetimes borders upon false hope. That is why he declared, *"I have a clear light now, free of all hocus-pocus."* Now, we should all strive for that selfsame clarity by taking him as the perfect exemplar.

"After getting exposed to the experiences of Kundalini of Sri Ramakrishna, and reading the Hindu/Indian commentators on Patanjala, I have become aware of the huge difference between gurus who court the physical world and body, and those who transmit dharmic teachings that open doors into all that is transcendent of matter and physical senses. The former claim to have realized Truth, Goddess, God, Consciousness, and other high ideals via the twin practices of stretching and breathing. They assert that Kundalini is awake in them, but never speak of or teach those austerities that, say, Sri Ramakrishna underwent to realize Mother Kali. And prana to them is just breathing. Am I wrong for thinking this way?"

I want more people to wake up to this facade perpetrated by both opportunists from India, and worldly Westerners seeking fame and money. There is no way that Mother Kundalini will awaken via cheap bribes like asanas. She requires pure love of Her and, as Sri Aurobindo has said, 100% commitment to Her. At one period of time in India people thought She would awaken via animal sacrifices in Her Name. That also proved to be wrong. Lord Buddha taught better and stood against that as well.

There is no intelligence in thinking that the physical can somehow rise or lead to the spiritual, just like sitting down and playing random keys on the piano day after day cannot lead to artistic mastery of that instrument. The body always proves an obstacle to realization unless it is transformed into a consecrated temple that humbly invites the Mother in. We must not give freedom to the senses; we must get freedom from the senses, and She will show us how. This is obvious to intelligent souls. But intelligence has gone missing in this day and age, has it not?

I can state that sitting with full attention in one posture (vajra or padma are best) can rouse one's udgata, but for this to occur one's attention must be on the mind's awareness, not on the asana). Udgata is a precursor to Kundalini. It is what beginners feel whenever the legs are spread in triangular cross-legged fashion, like with the American Indians who sat like that. It is primal. But the primal is very different from the spiritual. People in "flows of posture" are bound to imagine all sorts of things, and the bliss they feel in the physical nerves becomes both addicting and misleading. These are not yogis; these are bhogis. As the Great Master has said, *"The further one goes away from the world of name and form, the closer one gets to Brahman."*

Prana has no intelligence of its own. It is insentient. All sentience is in the Atman. As the prana is taken in and up with the breath it will come closer to Mother intelligence. Psychic prana is that connection. It (psychic prana) has not been introduced to the West. Neither have the Tanmatras. Swamiji found them both missing here, and their absence is the cause of practitioners here failing to reach a state of pure mind, and holding it.

These are much more than my thoughts; these are the teachings of beings who have realized nonduality and who are a whole cut different than those who came here from India armed with body-orientation masquerading as spirituality. The mistake (whether it was clever or just naive) of giving that to a materialistic culture, in our way of thinking, has blocked the spiritual nadis from opening here in the West rather than helping to open them.

"Thank you for your thoughtful reply. I accept what you say that true control of Prana is achieved with the mind. Yes, hatha fixes the mind for a period on the physical body, but might that be desirable to dissolve the granthis that affect our spiritual/mental/emotional well-being?"

Granthis form in the mind first, then come to the body, much like samskaras do. One dissolves them with mental and intellectual practices (sadhana) using the four great yogas to ensure that they do not appear in the body. I am so sorry, but asanas cannot dissolve granthis at their source, in the mind. They might help do so in the body, with muscles and such, but that helps only our physical well-being, not, as you write here, our "spiritual, mental, emotional well-being." Further, breaking apart even physical complexes utilizing physical practices only enhances one's misguided belief in the reality of what is physical, when "Only Brahman is Real."

Patanjali, the Father of Yoga, himself, has only one sutra in the Yoga Sutras about body postures. Swami Vivekananda and His Order have little to do with them (which is refreshing, actually), i.e., the swamis seldom practice them. His guru, Sri Ramakrishna, calls hatha yoga "bad," while Raja Yoga (Patanjala) He calls "good." Shankara criticizes hatha seriously. Sri Krishna never speaks of it in the Gita or elsewhere. The Mother scriptures limit it to two postures. The Upanisads seldom teach nor mention them. The Holy Mother states that it is not necessary for the serious sadhika to take them up. The Kundalini Yoga system also restricts them to two postures. Tantra, in general, allows for five postures. All of these references are by systems and beings who have foregone hatha yoga. It is not necessary, even for beginners, much less a habitual preoccupation with it over years.

"To my mind, the advantage of hatha is to be able to live out continuously one's sadhana with a healthy body that does not distract from one's spiritual practice over a longer period of time. As many have said, Enlightenment must be achieved while in a 3D physical body which is divine and contains the chakra-doorways to the spiritual realms. Correct me if I'm wrong."

Okay, yes: incorrect, or misleading, on several points. First, an obsession with physical health is exactly what distracts most beings today from spending a longer period of time on more authentic spiritual practices. Just look around and see.

Next, the chakras are not in the body; they rest in a much subtler set of ethers. Opportunists and sensationalists who know nothing other than body, breath, and baksheesh, have been teaching falsehoods like this since the 1960's. Chakras are inner worlds, vibrating spandas in the Great Mind. You cannot tune them with a tuning fork, straighten them with an asana, breathe them pure, or colorize them with an overactive imagination. These and other tactics are just ploys to attract followers and acquire their money; also to cause people to think that they are enlightened, when they are just pretentious opportunists.

If you want to know real Kundalini Yoga, read the Gospel of Sri Ramakrishna. He was/is the singular Great Master of Kundalini Yoga whose perfect teacher was Mother Kundalini Herself. Hard to argue with those credentials....

"Thank you for your responses on the subjects of hatha, prana, and Kundalini. Having said all that I did, I have to admit that in spite of decades of meditation practice I have yet to achieve samadhi, or what the Thervadans call jhana - so I could be entirely wrong! I'm open to changing my mind if I am convinced otherwise. You make some good points here, which I respect."

I am glad to note your openness and humility. Suffice to say that the Four Great Yogas - Jnanam, Bhakti, Raja, and Karma - are my main focus, and are what Swami Vivekananda brought out for seekers in this day and age. The West has not accepted them, and has gone for hatha instead. That alone should act as a warning sign for the materially-oriented, bodily-infatuated Westerner. The mind/psychic prana should be our guide, like it is for the luminary. The body/physical prana should duly and humbly follow that; then all will be well.

I will take this opportunity and opening in you to point out how some beings are born with spirituality intact, while others are either born without it, or have to try to develop it through lifetimes. That is due to mind mastery in a previous lifetime. The wise do not focus on the body, or on its good or ill health; they focus on Brahman and all else naturally rights itself. This is called watering the flowers and not the weeds in Vedanta - pratipakshabhavanam. Nonduality dawns in this same manner. Pretend nonduality and false attainment lodge themselves in the minds of those who take the body to be the soul, like sensualists, hedonists, and "spiritual materialists."

So, when you stated earlier that "Enlightenment must be achieved while in a 3D physical body which is divine and contains the chakra-doorways to the spiritual realms," all the seers would disagree, heartily. First of all Enlightenment is not "achieved," it is perceived; and secondly, as my guru used to say, "One cannot get to the eternal via the noneternal; one has to transcend the noneternal." That is because the noneternal is not real. Can one use the unreal to get to the Real? It is foolish thinking, really, contrary to the tradition and its philosophy. Further, we must realize the Ideal, not merely idealize the Real.

"During my contemplations and meditations I'm beginning to feel as if the five pranas are actually all aspects/forms of one Prana. This one Prana manifests itself in different ways according to what is to be done, but as one stills the mind and works on dissolving all thoughts into their source, the various functions of the pranas are no longer necessary and they return to the one Prana. Does this thinking make sense?"

In part. You only have to be careful around the "no longer necessary" declaration, for returning to things like the body, the world, helping others, denser levels of consciousness, etc., will require taking on the one, pervasive prana in its various forms. It is the same with other tattvas as well, like the ego.

Some think the ego dies and does not return. Actually, it deflates, ripens, and returns to host the consciousness of the one who is pressed into service by the Mother of prana, Herself. The old, tired argument about whether the ego is real or not is thus futile. It is there, then it is not, according to the Witness consciousness that may require it for embodiment in the various life-heavens, and even here on earth.

And essentially, nothing ever dies, because it was never actually born. Read and study your Gaudapada's Karika (with an adept teacher of nonduality). Everything is unoriginated. That is a declaration of Truth that blends Nonduality with Bliss. It is just that some things are more abiding than others. Divine Mother's prana is one of those. As the Prasnopanisad states about it, *"All created things were certainly present in the Divine Ether of Brahman's Heart before any inception. Like a hive of bees they were fashioned into individual souls, and thus came forth the different species."*

"The scriptures have many, many stories of asuras and rakshasas performing penance and meditating and winning boons. They can even become wise, like Ravana. Yet for all that effort, how do they so often turn it towards wicked ends? Does spiritual knowledge necessarily lead to insights and virtue, or is the knowledge neutral and thus lends itself to being misused and misapplied? Is it related to that saying, "Drink deep from the Well of Knowledge or don't drink at all;" or, "A little learning is a dangerous thing;" or, "You learn enough to hang yourself with"? Is it why our tradition discourages, for example, using drugs for spiritual insights, especially by Westerners? They're too likely to use the insights incorrectly? It seems to all loop back to the importance of a guru to help avoid pitfalls. Shamans taking searches on vision quests traditionally have been careful to make sure practitioners are qualified to take the trip and guide them, just like finding a guru to help guide you lest one's small ego get in the way and co-opt genuine insights. Or why book learning and philosophizing are not enough; they need to be married to practice and enlightened guidance to really bear good fruit."

Your second line of questioning is practically an answer for you. You understand the mayic nature of things here quite well. Suffice to say, further, that if one is qualified, has accomplished practices and matured the mind, then knowledge conduces to realization. Otherwise, the element of ignorance gets mixed in and spoils the broth. That is why Sri Krishna tells Arjuna: *"Knowledge that does not lead to Truth can be dangerous."* Even his righteous older brother, Yudhisthira, gambled, and that led to their involvement in the great war. We see these faults quite clearly in all runs of Western thought and act today; none of them are untouched by avidya. i.e., all of them are an admixture. Only spiritual knowledge will save, and it saves only if the mind that contemplates it is ready to imbibe it and realize it, is ready and committed to go the distance to Enlightenment with it. This month's set of Sunday classes is all about that qualification that is crucial to digest knowledge, transform it into wisdom, and then mature it into Truth.

Questions regarding problems in spiritual life may be directed to Nectar's editorial staff at: srvinfo@srv.org

◆ *Swami Aseshananda*

GOD AS MOTHER
The Feminine as the Dynamic Aspect of Brahman

Our eternal salutations to that one who is the truth of life and existence, and whom the devotees call by different names. Our eternal salutations to that one whose glories are sung in various hymns of the religious traditions of the world, but whose infinite and undying grandeur no mortal mind can comprehend. Our eternal salutations to that one upon whom the devotees meditate in the shrine of their hearts, realizing an ineffable presence in their deepest contemplations. May He prompt our minds towards the path of truth and righteousness. May he reveal himself unto our souls and dispel the gloom of death, fear, doubt and darkness. Om Peace, Peace, Peace. May Peace be unto us, may Peace be unto all of humanity.

The subject of my talk today is God as Mother. God as Mother is a beautiful concept. This concept is connected with the Advaita philosophy of the East. God as Father is connected with the dualistic philosophy which the West has accepted from the dawn of civilization.

The West thinks of dualism between man and God. Man is finite, and God is infinite. But when the East speaks about God as Mother it does not mean just the female principle, but the *shakti* aspect of Brahman. When I think of *Shakti*, divine energy, I think of Holy Mother. Holy Mother is the *Shakti*, is the *Janani*, the mother of our organization. Mother represents first, *advaita jnanam* — nondual experience of God in a transcendental state of Consciousness, which is beyond time, beyond space, beyond the law of causation. And in order to experience an exalted state of Consciousness where you will know your true nature. you will have to live a pure life.

So Mother, with whom God is associated, means purity of life. That is why Swami Abhedananda has written a poem:

pavitram charitam yasya pavitram jivanam tatha
pavitrata svarupinyai tasyai kurmo namo namah

"Noble is thy character, pure is your life divine, ever we bow to Thee, O Mother, Thou incarnate purity fine."

In order to understand purity of life, you have to turn the pages of Holy Mother's life. She never thought of anything which you can call worldliness, which brings selfishness, which brings attachment, which brings delusion to the mind. And therefore in order to think of Holy Mother, I go back to the days in which Holy Mother lived with Sri Ramakrishna.

One day Holy Mother was massaging his feet, and asked this question. Holy Mother looked upon Sri Ramakrishna as her guru. "How do you look upon me?" And Sri Ramakrishna said, immediately, *"The Mother that I have worshipped in the temple, is the same Mother who is now massaging my feet."*

And also, you will find, at the end of it all is *sadhana*. He performed a kind of ceremony. It is called, *Shodasi Puja*. Though *shodasi* means sixteen, Swami Saradananda came to know that she was eighteen at the time of that ceremony. Anyway, you look upon the wife not as wife, but as a symbol and expression of the dynamic aspect of *Brahman* — *Mahashakti*, or *Adyashakti*. When he offered his salutations to her, Sri Ramakrishna was in *samadhi*; Holy Mother was also in *samadhi*. In a normal state of consciousness Holy Mother would not have accepted worship from Sri Ramakrishna.

So we find that this age has brought a new inspiration to us. And that inspiration comes from the exalted life of Holy Mother. That is why the American people will send flowers to their own mother; very good. But why ordinary flowers? Send flowers of Love, flowers of devotion, you see.

But that is not enough. We have to think of what mother represents. Earthly mother can never give illumination, but Divine Mother can. Why should we worship the Divine Mother? Because, this idea stems from the idea of *Prakriti* and *Purusha* of the *Sankhya* philosophy. You have to search and find the Upanisadic days. For instance, the beautiful story of Yajnavalkya and Maitreyi; it comes twice. It is so important, and it is so meaningful, and it is so elevating.

Yajnavalkya wanted to renounce. Renounce, here, does not mean escaping; it was because his students wanted to become brahmacharis and monks. Yajnavalkya and Maitreyi lived like brother and sister, called *vanaprastin* life. At the age of 65, husband and wife retire to a forest, and they live a life of renunciation blended with contemplation of God. So, he thought within himself, I cannot teach monasticism unless I become a monk myself. So he went to ask permission of his wife, for there should be mutual agreement. I have lived this kind of life for more than 60 years, so I can speak from my conviction. I cannot give this teaching of monasticism to the householders...well, a little, perhaps, not too much (laughter). Domestic harmony is necessary. You should not split the bondage created by God....well, not really bondage (loud and long laughter). Help is necessary in life.

So Yajnavalkya wanted the permission of his wife. Then Maitreyi said, *"What will happen to me?"* He replied, *"I have left you sufficient money; you will be able to live a good and comfortable life."* Then Maitreyi asked this question, *"Can money and comfort bring immortality, because you will attain immortality, and I also want to attain immortality."* He answered, *"No."* Through material values alone you can never attain spiritual wisdom; they cannot give you freedom; cannot give you enlightenment. In order to attain enlightenment you will have to build your own character upon a firm foundation. And you must have the power to resist things that will assail your consciousness and try to bring you down from the higher ideals of life. And that is why he told her that in order to attain immortality she will have to purify her heart and transcend the limitations of the senses, as well as the limitations of the intellect.

What is the limitation of the intellect in the intellectual frame of reference? That limitation is the limitation of creating a distinction between subject and object. Also, it is the intellect that brings time, space, and causation. If you accept time to be real, you will have to suffer time as if it were real as well. If you accept space, you will have to think in terms of your limited body, your limited form.

Swami Vivekananda has come to enlighten you, to awaken you, to take you home, to give you strength, to give you energy, to give you enthusiasm, and to give you the invaluable pearl of great price which I call jivanmukti. That is freedom in this life with this body.

Dualistic philosophy has never mentioned it, neither in the East nor in the West. It is only the nondualistic philosophy of Shankara or Gaudapada that speaks of it, and so eloquently. It is not the philosophy of reason alone; it is the philosophy that is based upon personal experience in *nirvikalpa samadhi*.

And Sri Ramakrishna's great *sadhana* will reveal that, because he first practiced dualistic philosophy of life to experience the personal God under the guidance of Bhairavi Brahmani. But

> "You have hypnotized yourself into thinking that you are a finite individual, limited individual, precarious individual, lost in this wilderness of the world. You are thinking in the wrong way, and Swami Vivekananda has come to enlighten you, to awaken you, to take you home, to give you strength, to give you energy, to give you enthusiasm, and to give you the invaluable pearl of great price which I call *jivanmukti*. That is freedom in this life with this body."

If you accept the law of causation to be real, you will have to accept death. Probably, your hope will be going to heaven. But that hope may not be a real hope. The real hope of mankind will appear when one transcends time, space, and causation. That will only happen when you purify your intellect.

This is the reason why Yajnavalkya told Maitreyi, "*It is not for the sake of the husband that the husband is dear, but for the sake of the Eternal Soul that the husband is dear. It is not for the sake of the wife that the wife is dear, but for the sake of the Eternal Soul that the wife is dear.*" Then he gave her an example, saying, if one puts a lump of salt in water it dissolves. Similarly, when a man or women transcends time, space, and causation and realizes God, he or she will go beyond all the limitations of the senses, and the intellect, and realize his or her true nature to be infinite existence, infinite knowledge, and infinite bliss.

Then, he concluded, that when this enlightenment comes, individuality is no more. Then Maitreyi became frightened, and said, "*If enlightenment comes and my individuality goes away, I will become nothing. You have confused me.*" Then he said, "*I have not come to confuse you; you have simply not understood properly. What I mean to say is that your spurious, false, limited individuality will be no more. But your real individuality is connected with infinite truth, infinite beauty, and infinite goodness that will never go away, because being transcendent of time, space, and causality It has no beginning, It has no end. So you are to think of yourself not as a wave floating in the ocean of time, you have to think of yourself as the whole ocean.*" This was the timeless and eternal message that Yajnavalkhya gave to Maitreyi.

And that is the message that I preach to the American people. You have hypnotized yourself into thinking that you are a finite individual, limited individual, precarious individual, lost in this wilderness of the world. You are thinking in the wrong way, and

Totapuri, an Advaitic monk who experienced *nirvikalpa samadhi* by meditating for forty years, came on the scene. He told Sri Ramakrishna, "*You would be a good student of Advaita Vedanta; do you want to be my student?*" Sri Ramakrishna said, "*I will have to ask my teacher.*" But Bhairavi Brahmani said "No." She did not give him permission, but told him that if he followed that teaching of *Advaita Vedanta* his devotion would disappear, and he would become a dry monk.

But Sri Ramakrishna did not listen. He went to the temple of the Divine Mother — who is the *Antaryami*, the inner ruler immortal seated in the heart — and She gave him permission to practice *Advaita sadhana*. The difficulty that Sri Ramakrishna had was to withdraw his mind from the blissful form of the Divine Mother. But, the instruction of Totapuri was that he had to transcend the realm of the personal God, and to transcend his attachment to the pure ego. The pure ego is a gold chain; you have to break all fetters, all chains. And so the story says, that he used the sword of discrimination and cut away the form of the Mother and his mind soared to the transcendent realm beyond. He lost all outer consciousness but he was filled with the Consciousness of the infinite Spirit as the Life of his life, as the Soul of his soul, as the Essence of his being.

So here you find the *maya*. The *mayavada* of Shankara is interpreted by many people in a wrong way. The *mayavada* of Shankara is very similar to the relativity theory of Einstein. Newton accepted time, space, and causation to be absolute reality, but not Einstein. It is Einstein who proved mathematically that they are all relative — the space/time continuum. But Einstein did not accept the law of causation to also be relative. Whatever it may be, it is not by the objective method, but it is purity of life that is necessary to help one transcend the limitations of the senses and the intellect.

> "And therefore, I call a guru a specialist, because he knows the nature of the human mind. Mind has a rajasic nature, an outgoing nature. It needs to be controlled. Without self-control one cannot attain self-mastery, and without self-mastery one cannot attain self-realization. And without self-realization one cannot be a *jivanmukta*."

And therefore, it is Holy Mother's life that is an example of spiritual energy that cannot be realized unless one leads a pure life, living the life of a Universal Mother, and for spreading the message of wisdom, as well as the message of compassion to the rest of mankind. She accepted men and women, irrespective of creed, color, nationality, and race, as her own children

And that is the reason why we have to think of her and her exemplary life. Divine Mother stands for two real important things: one, She is the source of the creation, preservation, and destruction of the universe. That is called the dynamic aspect of *Brahman*. And then there is also the transcendent aspect of *Brahman*. These are the *Saguna* aspect and the *Nirguna* aspects.

But *prakriti* of the Shankara view is unconscious, so until we overcome *maya* and attachment to the world one has to worship God as Mother, which means *Mahamaya*. What is the definition of *Mahamaya* according to Shankara? She who makes the impossible possible. Man thinks that it is impossible for him to realize God in this life. But Divine Mother comes and says, *"No, through My Grace it will be possible."*

And therefore, there is Her Grace. Vedanta does not speak so eloquently about Grace, but the *Tantra Shastras* speak about Grace. And therefore, this Grace is connected with what is called *Kundalini Shakti*. In every person there is what is called infinite energy, but it is lying asleep in most. The scientist, for example, is also worshipping Mother, but only in Her material and mechanical aspects. By splitting the atom, infinite energy has been realized, but for what purpose? To blow out the world. Sri Ramakrishna has awakened the Mother, but in Her conscious aspect, *Chit-shakti*; *Brahma-shakti*. And by awakening the *Chit-shakti* he has done immense good to mankind by giving everyone strength, energy, power, delight, as well as immortality of the Soul.

And that is the reason why when I think of Divine Mother, I think of *Kundalini Shakti*. It has nothing to do with the female principle; it has nothing to do with material society, it is *Shakti*. *Shakti* is energy, but energy can be unconscious. It is the conscious energy that cannot be realized unless one lives a pure life.

The concept of Mother is connected with renunciation, is connected with meditation, is connected with realization in *savikalpa samadhi*, as well as in *nirvikalpa samadhi*. So when I think of Holy Mother, I think of Mother as the *Guru*. What is the meaning of the word *Guru*? Dispeller of darkness. Who can dispel darkness? The person who is enlightened. Otherwise it will just be the blind leading the blind. Similarly, will intellectual understanding alone transform life? Transformation of life only comes when one comes into contact with an illumined soul, and accepts this awakened human soul as one's own *guru*.

Therefore, Mother represents *guru-shakti*. *Guru-shakti* comes from realization of God in *samadhi*. Again, one should follow the instruction of the *guru* through the *mantra*. One has to cultivate faith in the *mantra*.

A disciple came to the Mother, and Mother said, *"I have given the mantra; repeat the mantra with firm faith and devotion, and gradually, when the mind becomes pure, you will be able to know the benefits of spiritual life."* And therefore, I call a *guru* a specialist, because he knows the nature of the human mind. Mind has a *rajasic* nature, an outgoing nature. It needs to be controlled. Without self-control one cannot attain self-mastery, and without self-mastery one cannot attain Self-realization. And without Self-realization one cannot be a *jivanmukta*. One cannot think I am free and have it be the truth; be free from the bonds and anxieties of this mundane material and transitory life.

And that is the reason why the subconscious mind must be pure. Only an illumined soul can help with that, not a professional therapist whose own mind is still impure. And certainly not your own ego who has led you into trouble time and time again. It is well-guided spiritual practice that makes the difference. Practice a little. What does practice mean? Take for example that I want to bring electricity here, into this room. I will not do it myself; I will go to an electrician. But this electrician must not just know a little; he must be a contractor with a license. He will tell me, "These wires are not safe, Swami. I have to put new ones in. I must replace these wires. And you must pay me $600." (laughter)

Anyway, as I need strong wires, similarly I need strong knobs. And self-control has that. Not self-expression. In that you fritter away your energy. Enjoyment saps the energy of the senses, depletes the mind, and man becomes lost in the wilderness of this world. The religion of strength comes through self-control.

Gandhi? I have seen Gandhi. Other politicians, they did not create any influence, but when Gandhi came into the picture he created great influence. That is because he practiced self-control. And what he practiced, he preached.

Similarly, religion is not just merely giving a lecture. Religion means building one's own life on a strong foundation. Christ said, do not build your house on sand, build your house on a rock. So the moral principles are to be accepted, ethical values have to be accepted. We call this *dharma* — righteous living.

But righteous living is not the ultimate goal. The ultimate goal of human existence is immortality. It is not salvation. Salvation is only a post-mortem emancipation. And therefore I agree with Shankaracharya. One has to attain *jivanmukti*. You have to transcend the intellectual plane of consciousness and reach the transcendental plane which the Hindus call *samadhi*. Buddhists call it *nirvana*. Some mystic Christians call it Beatific Vision. But even in such a vision there is dualism; dualism between the individual soul and the universal soul. Therefore,

> "When we think of the method we think of Sri Ramakrishna. When we think of Grace we think of Holy Mother. Mother is the embodiment of infinite power, but also the embodiment of infinite compassion."

beatific vision is not sufficient. It must be *nirvikalpa samadhi*. There is not the slightest trace of dualism in it. That is why Swamiji longed for only one thing: *nirvikalpa samadhi*.

When he was going to deposit his fees for his law examination, *vairagya* came, renunciation came. Renunciation does not mean condemnation. The real meaning of renunciation is deification. The husband will see the Divine Mother in the wife, and wife will see Lord Siva in the husband. Mother here means the Atman. In *Atman* there is no distinction between husband and wife. There is only one thing in *Atman*: the Infinite — infinite strength, infinite life, infinite beauty, and infinite wisdom. It is indivisible Consciousness.

So you cannot reach the infinite Consciousness without attaining transcendence of the senses and the limitations of the intellect. Also, the limitations of the idea of individual soul and the Universal Soul. The West has rejected, for instance, Meister Ekhart. Meister Ekhart has spoken about this nondualism when he says that, "*The eye with which man sees God is the same eye with which God sees man.*"

This nondualistic experience is the special gift of Eastern philosophers like Nagarjuna, who first propounded that the law of causation is relative, then, Gaudapada, when he spoke of *ajata*, or noncausality; then Shankara as *mayavada*. In *mayavada* you think that name and form are real, but as long as you accept this you will never be able to be fully conscious of your true nature. He used the words *nama*, *rupa*, and *svarupa*. When your vision is distorted you accept name and form to be real; that is called *maya*.

Shankara's view is *mayavada*, but I would call it *Brahmavada ekatavada*. That is the positive way of speaking about it. When you talk about *mayavada* that is the cloud. When you ask the question how the One has become the many, how the infinite has become the finite, how the absolute has become the relative, that is all in *parinamavada*. You are stuck thinking that the law of causation is the ultimate reality.

The book of Genesis speaks about it as well, that God created the world out of nothing, and God created individual souls. But as long as you accept this law of creation to be the final word, you cannot accept immortality, nor the divinity of man nor of the soul to be real. So causation is also a relative truth. Because there is apparent change in the Infinite. That is called by Aris-to-tal — excuse me, my pronunciation is Calcutta pronunciation (laughter) but try to understand (more laughter) — okay, what Aristotle called the "unmoved mover." That means, God is infinite, but being the Ultimate Reality, His presence and proximity has produced all these changes. Shankara calls this *vivarta*, that all changes come from the mind, and then mind superimposes them on Ultimate Reality. It is rather like watching a movie, that is, all the changes take place on the film, not on the silent screen.

For instance, I heard President Reagan say that his time is over. But that is not true. Time in the White House is over, but time in the rest of the world goes on. So time is a category of the mind and a power of the intellect. Here you are under the hypnotism that *vritti-chaitanya* is actual, that the waves of the mind are somehow real. Here, the background is the ego, not the *Atman*. So you have to transcend the individual frame of reference and practice detachment. If you practice detachment, then your reality is not connected with the changing phenomena of the universe, or the changing moods of the mind, but with the Witness Consciousness behind them. And that Witness Consciousness that Shankaracharya is always talking about is the *nitya-chaitanya*, the Eternal Consciousness.

And going back to it, that is what Yajnavalkya told Maitreyi, that the consciousness of the seer never goes away. That is because it is a property, not a quality — just like the sun is always shining, since sun and its shining power go together. It is an invariable characteristic. But the moon shines by borrowed light. Similarly, mind and intellect are not conscious by their own power, but borrow the power of illumination from the *Atman*.

Now, if the question arises that *Atman* borrows light from God, no, it is not possible, because when you are referencing the Infinite, the Infinite is always nondual. It is partless; it is not a compound thing. Inside of the law of causation, the Infinite is bound to change, but a changeful infinite is no infinite at all. The Infinite is that which must be changeless at all times, and under all circumstances.

The dialectic materialism of Russia always speaks of matter that changes. Democratic West has accepted Spirit that changes. But we in India follow Shankaracharya and reveal the Spirit that suffers no possibility of change, because Spirit is the *Atman*. *Atman* does not know birth, does not know death. *Atman* does not go to heaven, does not reincarnate. *Atman* is all-pervading Consciousness.

Westerners have hypnotized themselves and forgotten their real nature as *Atman*. They have lost the real Paradise. But we can regain that ultimate Paradise, the Paradise of Freedom, when we become detached from our psycho-physical being which is eternal Spirit, unbounded freedom, perennial joy, infinite wisdom, and infinite love.

That infinite wisdom represents Sri Ramakrishna. That infinite love represents Holy Mother. And that is the reason why, Holy Mother said to Swami Vivekananda, "*Go to the West and preach the message of the Master.*" And she thus gave him her blessing. This blessing is called the Grace of the Mother.

When we think of the method we think of Sri Ramakrishna. When we think of Grace we think of Holy Mother. Mother is the embodiment of infinite power, but also the embodiment of infinite compassion. Swami Turiyananda used to say that it is difficult to please Sri Ramakrishna because he thinks in terms of precision, but the Mother can be pleased. Why? Because she is *karunamayi*. It means full of compassion.

A girl came to me from Sacramento. She said, you have seen Holy Mother. Please tell me about Holy Mother. I told her to read the books. But she was not satisfied. She said please tell me something. So I said, when the whole world rejects you, and then you turn your mind to the Holy Mother, She will accept you. And she will never fail you at any moment of your life.

When I came to this country, to New York, there was a blizzard. It was 1947. I wondered if I would be able to adjust to this country. Several times I wanted to go back, but the Divine Mother said to *"be patient. The grace of Sri Ramakrishna will come; he will protect you. He will be your guide."* And so here, coming to Portland, I have Holy Mother. Holy Mother is our guide, and the undying source of our inspiration.

And further, there are two things man needs for success. One is called money, and another, manpower. Money, we have got. The second, Manpower....we have to be patient. Manpower is very difficult to get, because in Vedanta we preach renunciation. We have to test people in order to find out if they can be stable, and steady. But with Divine Mother's Grace, all things are possible.

And that is the reason why, on this Mother's Day, we need the *karuna* aspect of Divine Mother. The *Shakti* aspect of the Mother we need for *sadhana*, but the *karuna* aspect of the Mother we need for enlightenment. And that is the message that you find in the *Chandi*, or *Durga Saptasati*. *Saptasati* means seven verses connected with the glory of the Divine Mother. There, you hear that when the Divine Mother becomes *varada*, the giver, and is pleased, she gives the boon of protection. She disarms all fears from the minds of her children and brings fearlessness.

And that is why the concept of Mother is also connected with death. In Vedanta we do not accept dualistic principles. For instance, that saying, *"the wages of sin is death."* That means all good things come from God, and all things that are undesirable come from another force, called Lucifer, or Satan. No, the truth is that the world is *maya*. Good and evil are the two sides of the same coin. Similarly, are pleasure and pain, and life and death. You have to transcend dualities. And you have to accept in order to transcend. Death is not an enemy; death is a friend. Because when death comes we have to finally think of Mother. We have to meditate on the Mother. And that is my message to all of you here on Mother's Day.

And so, *"May peace come unto all, may knowledge dawn upon all, may all see the face of Truth, and be fortified by the armor of Love. Om Peace, Peace, Peace.*
May peace be unto us,
May peace be unto all.
Hari Om, Hari Om,
Hari Om Tat Sat."

Swami Aseshananda, a direct disciple of Sri Sarada Devi, Sri Ramakrishna's wife and spiritual consort, was the Spiritual Minister of the Vedanta Society of Portland for over forty years. He also received holy company with some of the direct disciples of the Great Master. He is the author of Glimpses of a Great Soul, on the life and teachings of Swami Saradananda.

Ramprasad Poem

Mother dwells at the center of my being,
forever delightfully at play.
Whatever conditions of consciousness arise,
I hear the music of Her Holy Names....
Om Tara. Om Durga, Om Kali.

Closing my eyes, I perceive the Wisdom
Mother dancing in the lotus of my heart.
She wears a garland of skulls, emblem of
Her freedom from birth and death.
Gazing upon Her radiant nakedness,
mundane concepts and conventions vanish
and those who judge by mundane
standards call me mad.

Timid and limited persons can think
whatever they wish
My only longing is to express the total
madness of Divine Love.

This precocious child of the Goddess
cries out with abandon:
"The Queen of the Universe resides
in the flower of my secret heart."

Mother, Mother, Mother!
I seek refuge at Your beautiful Lotus Feet.
As my body dissolves into earth,
may I dissolve into You.

(Translation by Lex Hixon)

THE DIRE EFFECTS OF VISMRITI
The Root Causes for Loss of Divine Memory Over Lifetimes

Alzheimer's, move over! Either move over, or reveal the primal cause of yourself. For, enlightened souls know that all diseases spring from the mind. They exist there in potential after birth on earth take place. Germs? These are just negative thoughts in the mind getting ready to fructify. Remedies? They are merely afterthoughts formed due to the misassumption that illness is real. Perfect Health? That is pure mind, and it is enjoyed by the luminaries as the true nature of *Atman*. And the best immune system? It is constant thought of and concentration upon *Brahman*. As one divine hymn of Mother India puts it: *"Oh mind; do not forget to remember your Mother Durga's precious Name."*

The origin of Mother India's originless teaching of divine memory, i.e., *daiva smriti*, is best traced back to the time of Ramachandra and his wisdom teacher, Lord Vasishtha. The Lord states, in his story about King Shikidvaja in the *Nirvana Prakarana* of the scripture, *Yoga Vasishtha*, that all disease originates in the mind. The reasons he gives for this unacceptable loss are: rebirth in the body accompanied by lack of discriminating wisdom; want of mastery over the senses in a previous lifetime, and the inability to stem desires rising in the mind also lacking in a past lifetime. One could very astutely conclude, then, that for the spiritually unawakened soul, rebirth is the very first disease; all the others come in its train.

Import of the Doctrine of Rebirth

Legions of fine teachings could be listed about divine memory from India's storehouse of scriptures, but this article is about its loss and what causes it. The chart on the next page gives both the causes for its absence in life today, and several unique spiritual practices that allow the soul to reclaim it. Unfortunately, one great hurdle in this task is Western man's failure to either believe in past births, or look into the art of rebirth. India, Tibet, China, Japan, and other countries still hold rebirth as a relative truth. A few religions hold it as the absolute truth, but that is due, ironically enough, to their loss of memory of *samadhi*, *nirvana*, *satori*, etc., which are names for the singular state of nondual Self-Realization. The *advaitic* teaching that outstrips that knowledge of the wheel of rebirth is the fact that the Soul is unoriginated, is unborn (*ajati*). But that is crucial material for another article. To reclaim perennial wisdom today, and utilize it for everything from healing to illumination of mind, we must begin with the *karmic* tendencies that robbed the incarnating soul of its memory of previous births in the first place, as well as all that it learned there.

The Forgetful Individual's List of Un-Redressable Grievances

Ironically, again, and very tedious to contemplate, is the predicament that the embodied soul lets itself in for when it arrives on earth (from the heavens of the mind) and falls pedantically into repeating everything it did in its last body and birth. To do so via forgetting all the schooling, all the lessons, all the sufferings, and all the attainments that it won for itself previously is verily unthinkable. On top of this great oversight, and as the chart on the next page begins to show us, is the problem of being born in an *adharmic* society peopled by parents who, ignorant of anything other than matter and how to secure it, route young souls towards materialism and the pleasures it is supposed to give, what Swami Vivekananda called *"the eternal moneymaking."* For as the chart relates next, these worldly souls, imbued with forgetfulness, were born due to their thirst (*trishna*) for exploring and conquering external worlds. Their *samskaras*, or past-life impressions, bind them to caste, class, convention, families, and wealth-based occupations that they lived and relived for countless lifetimes over the period of an age. Nary a one ever awoke from such a self-actuated trap, and it is doubtful that such souls ever will. This is called "mass-collective mental dreaming" by the seers, and is the very definition of the Sanskrit word, *sankalpa*.

Thus far, and according to the chart herein, the causes of wrong orientation, thirst for embodied existence, past-life mental impressions, and attachment to wealth and its various ways of usage, erode and veil the memory of incarnating souls. There are reasons on the cosmic level as well, but these will be viewed and discussed later in this article. Suffice to say, that what is called the *eshanatrayam*, the triple bondage of spouse, offspring, and objects of desire, figures into the obliteration of a being's deeper memory of past lifetimes. Another heavy overlay in the process, as is concurred by Buddhism in its Four Noble Truths and Twelve *Nidanas* systems, is the presence of suffering. It is not so much the pain one has to go through that is the impediment, but rather the slow-brewing thought that suffering is actual. The pain (*dukha*) which one forbears passes; what remains is the memory of it that causes fear of it, that then finally implants it in the mind's subconscious. As instanced by souls who have bliss rather than suffering as their mind's substratum, the simultaneous grasping after pleasure and receiving of pain, in turn, runs a deep furrow in the ordinary mind's memory. The saints and seers suffer, no doubt, but the shield of love and devotion to God, what to speak of higher wisdom, resists the formation of mental impressions in them, and also allows them glimpses of Reality — with form and beyond form — at times.

Additionally, there are some kinds of suffering that do not merely pass off; that is, they stay with the process of life and insinuate themselves upon it constantly. *Sadurmi*, also spoken of as the six transformations in Indian philosophy, wreak an almost invisible violence on the weakened human mind. Birth, growth, disease, old age, decay, and death, along with contributing factors like

The Dire Effects of Vismriti
Causes For Loss Of Divine Memory Over Lifetimes

"Unillumined minds project their crystalized mental complexes into numerous bodies over cycles of time. With the exception of souls possessing resilient memories, passing through the curtain of nescience between the realm of the ancestors and the earth plane strips all past-life remembrances from them." — Babaji Bob Kindler

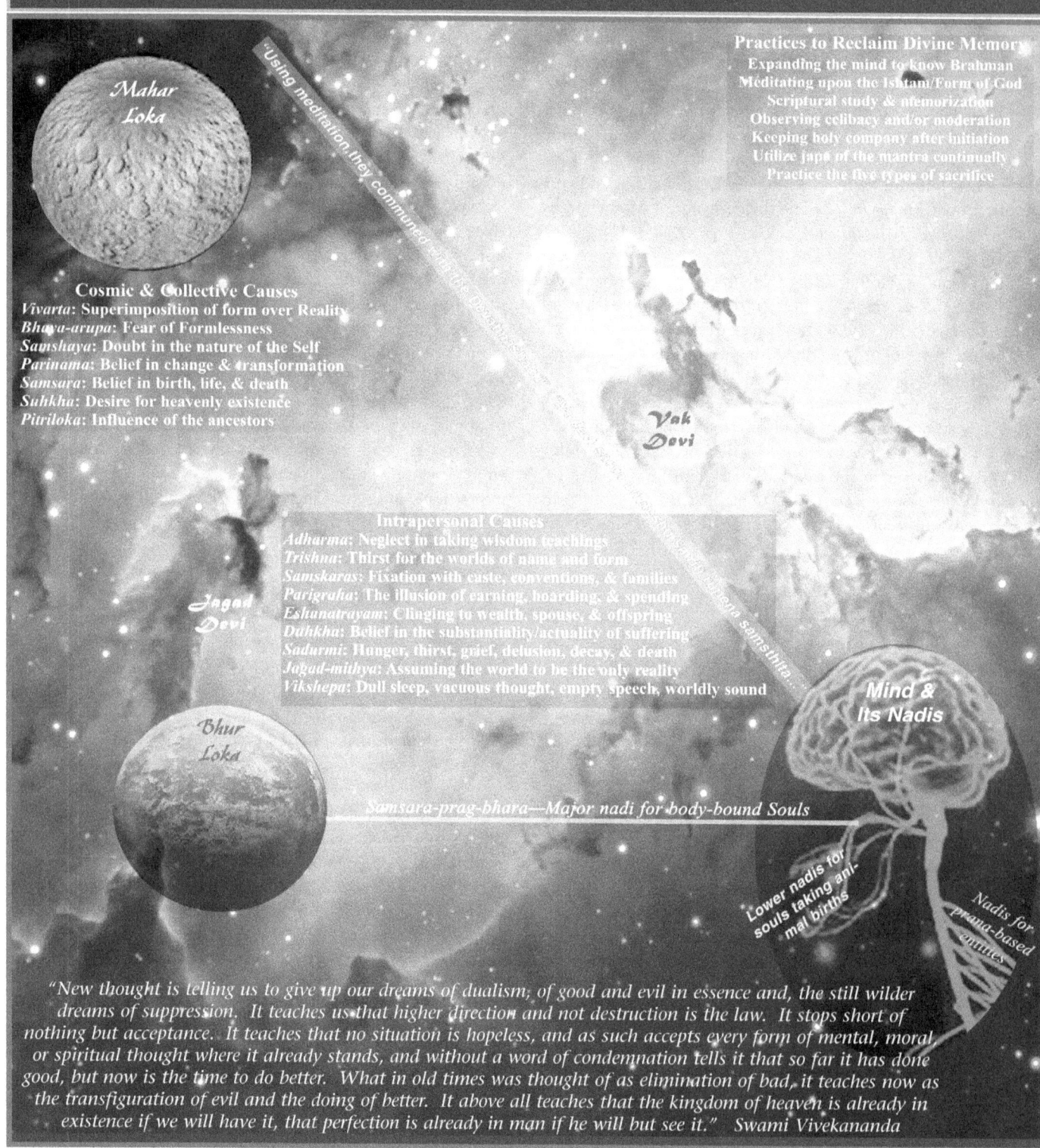

Mahar Loka

"Using meditation they communed with the Devatas..."

Practices to Reclaim Divine Memory
Expanding the mind to know Brahman
Meditating upon the Ishtam/Form of God
Scriptural study & memorization
Observing celibacy and/or moderation
Keeping holy company after initiation
Utilize japa of the mantra continually
Practice the five types of sacrifice

Cosmic & Collective Causes
Vivarta: Superimposition of form over Reality
Bhaya-arupa: Fear of Formlessness
Samshaya: Doubt in the nature of the Self
Parinama: Belief in change & transformation
Samsara: Belief in birth, life, & death
Suhkha: Desire for heavenly existence
Pitriloka: Influence of the ancestors

Vak Devi

...hridaye chaiva sarvasya samsthita

Intrapersonal Causes
Adharma: Neglect in taking wisdom teachings
Trishna: Thirst for the worlds of name and form
Samskaras: Fixation with caste, conventions, & families
Parigraha: The illusion of earning, hoarding, & spending
Eshanatrayam: Clinging to wealth, spouse, & offspring
Duhkha: Belief in the substantiality/actuality of suffering
Sadurmi: Hunger, thirst, grief, delusion, decay, & death
Jagad-mithya: Assuming the world to be the only reality
Vikshepa: Dull sleep, vacuous thought, empty speech, worldly sound

Jagad Devi

Mind & Its Nadis

Bhur Loka

Samsara-prag-bhara—Major nadi for body-bound Souls

Lower nadis for souls taking animal births

Nadis for prana-based entities

"New thought is telling us to give up our dreams of dualism, of good and evil in essence and, the still wilder dreams of suppression. It teaches us that higher direction and not destruction is the law. It stops short of nothing but acceptance. It teaches that no situation is hopeless, and as such accepts every form of mental, moral, or spiritual thought where it already stands, and without a word of condemnation tells it that so far it has done good, but now is the time to do better. What in old times was thought of as elimination of bad, it teaches now as the transfiguration of evil and the doing of better. It above all teaches that the kingdom of heaven is already in existence if we will have it, that perfection is already in man if he will but see it." — Swami Vivekananda

hunger and thirst, are all painful, even beyond the physical. Whether life is accompanied by riches or poverty, health or illness, provisions or none, all suffer from these transformations as they occur in various combinations.

The last two elements for the cause for loss of memory in the individual, bridge upon the cosmic level of debilitation, sometimes called "despoilers" in *Yoga*. Blind ignorance, combined with the complete lack of ability in most souls to train themselves in the arts of moderation and detachment, combine to convince the mind of *jagad-mithya*, the false perspective that the world is actual, i.e., the only reality. Experiences gained from matter, objects, and senses, all ignited to burn faster and longer by the emotional heart's ill-guided search for pleasures, bring about this skewed and twisted world-view. Instead of the noble, true-life giving fervor and virility that balanced life will give to the soul, this animalistic path is taken with. The term, "intelligent ignorance," might be coined here, or ignorant intelligence. With a changing mind in an ever-changing world, modern savants and worldly-wise beings of the recent past looked out to find phenomena, only. The stationary Subject always and ever escaped their attention, because all that was unstationary (consisting of changing particles) constantly averted their attention from It.

Thus, one of the underlying lynchpins for human ignorance is belief in change, or *parinama* in Sanskrit. The human soul, when it gets into the body, intensely wants to explore worlds of name and form in time and space. This desire, or heavenly wanderlust, is based upon *vismriti*, loss of memory. Forgetting that all worlds (and their resources), all objects (and the pleasures they give), and all beings (and the friendship they afford), are within the Self (Essence/Atman), they produce bodies with their spiritually

> "Beings do not realize that the Infinite cannot be gained through the finite. It is gained only by seeing through the finite, which is unreal (empty, substanceless) to begin with."

up, and its pursuit weakens the natural immune system that otherwise keeps retentive memory active, and availed of a many lifetime longevity. The last entry listed on the chart under intrapersonal causes of loss of memory then becomes the ongoing resort. Termed *vikshepa* in true *Yoga* practice, the now physically drained and spiritually complacent *jiva* falls into a life of vacuous thoughts, empty speech, meaningless entertainment, and dull sleep.

Cosmic and Collective Causes for Lack of Retentive Memory

To look deeper — and the intrepid soul seeking freedom from all bondage must do so — subtle causes which lie at a very deep level of mind (subconscious/unconscious) are to be traced and neutralized. These are culminative. They lurk and linger at causal levels, and manifest in successive lifetimes, falsely appearing to be of the natural run of things. Attachment to form, for instance, and later, fear of the formless, settle in. When the soul is born in a body, name and form have already become the norm to the mind and its thinking process. When habit around this primal error coagulates as mental concepts, forgetfulness of the perfect, formless, nameless Essence of humanity, sets in. Thus, false superimposition (*vivarta*), fear of uncovering the veiled truth (*bhaya-arupa*), and doubt that truth ever existed (*samshaya*) in the first place, work together.

It will be difficult for the human mind, beleaguered as it is by so many false and mixed conditionings, to wake up to all that has happened to it over time, and over lifetimes. A well-developed intelligence, as the seers state, will be necessary, and this intelligence is not mainly of the secular and worldly-wise kind. Matter, as has already been revealed, is a false imposition over human Essence (Atman), so utilizing it as a starting ground for spiritual awakening (if materialists were even interested in the Spirit) and all that follows, is a dead-end. Beings do not realize that the Infinite cannot be gained through the finite. It is gained only by seeing through the finite, which is unreal (empty, substanceless) to begin uninformed minds and venture out. Some become so enamored of the external nonessence, and so forgetful of their true home (Brahman/God), that they rotate in extended cycles (*samsara*) of time for ages. This is really the heart of the meaning of *vismriti*, i.e., fascination with nature (produced by the mind) combined with — as Shankara states it — neglect of remembering *Brahman*.

The last three cosmic causes of *vismriti*, listed on the chart under scrutiny, are related to the soul's belief in "real" change, in the appearance of transformation. For birth, life, and death are changes, taken on and engaged with inside of the illusion of change. And leaving the body and returning to it also involves changes taking place, so death does not relieve the burden of action, *karma*, and often adds to it. Religion, in its more fundamentalist stance, even fosters the idea of constant change in the soul, pointing it to heaven as the goal of existence. But the goal of human existence is Formless, is transcendental, like its ultimate "location." As Swami Vivekananda has stated, *"Coming and going is all pure delusion. The soul never comes nor goes. Where is the place to which it shall go, when all of space is in the soul? When shall be the time of entering or departing, when all time is in the soul?"*

It is the ever-stationary Self, then, that all beings must epitomize. It is That which all beings, once having lost It, seek. It is also That in which all embodied beings play, and until memory of That returns, sometime within the play of the Infinite Spirit, its dream-play will be attended by the pain of separation and subject to forgetfulness. As the Great Swami writes, again: *"The whole secret is that a man gives up the old garment he was wearing, and is standing where he was through all eternity. Will he manifest another such garment in this or any other world? I sincerely pray that he may not, not until he does so in full consciousness."*

The last two cosmic causes for the regretful, risky, and ofttimes painful forgetfulness of the Divine, which is our very Self, are the questionable goals of heavenly existence and the influence of our ancestors. The Light of Brahman, this inmost Self, is formless, say the illumined seers. The "space" of It is infinite, not com-

> "For the Illumined, if they embody at all, they spend their time in spiritual disciplines (*sadhana*), meditation (*dhyana yoga*), conscious deep sleep (*mahanidra*), and peaceful contemplation of Divine Reality (*shantatma*). The worldly do not even have names for these sweet and subtle occupations."

partmentalized. The "time" in It is endless, not incrementalized. It is Ultimate and untouchable, even by the mind. To "touch It" one would need to manifest nature and senses. With even this much acknowledged, it can be seen how realms such as "heavenly spheres" and forms such as "dearly-departed ones" would not be present There. Heaven and celestial beings are the goal of earthbound beings, then, not of freedom-seeking souls or beings that are already liberated from all this *maya*. For the bound, incarnating over and over again throughout dream-like cycles of linearized time only runs the hazy habits of birth and death further into the mind. This error, combined with all the other intrapersonal and cosmic conditionings that have been discussed earlier in this article, results in the overall forgetfulness of the nameless, formless, timeless, spaceless, Reality, i.e., one's own Self, *Atman*.

For the dreamers, time spent on a mentally conceptualized planet in insentient space far outweighs time spent in peaceful formlessness. They court the fleeting happiness of heaven and earth (*sukha*) rather than the unending Bliss of the Spirit (*ananda*). For the Illumined, if they embody at all, they spend their time in spiritual disciplines (*sadhana*), meditation (*dhyana yoga*), conscious deep sleep (*mahanidra*), and peaceful contemplation of Divine Reality (*shantatma*). The worldly do not even have names for these sweet and subtle occupations. Another way to "pass time in the body" for the seers, is to dwell in timelessness, in what is called, "The Eternal Moment." Even if acts are initiated in this realm-less realm, no repercussions of any kind come back from them. All acts done "in time" are replete with returns, with *karmas* that lead to more of the same, with chains. Acting while not acting, moving while not moving, thinking while not thinking – these are some of the "pastimes" of the illumined souls. As the scriptures of Mother India relate about them,

"She, who is known and remembered by the seers to be the Imperishable Shakti, is the very soul of the sutras and slokas of the revealed scriptures of India. Without Her, oh fair one, All the tattvas would be like clouds with no rain. She is the perfect I-Consciousness inherent in the multitude of words, And the secret of all the sacred mantras. Whose very nature is the essence of Nonduality. AUM Peace, Peace, Peace.

The Reclamation of Divine Memory

As the chart under study reveals, there is good news for those who sincerely desire to awaken to their own perfect nature. It involves the seeker's strong desire to expand the mind out of self-imposed limitations. Impediments of the cosmic variety cannot be challenged and overcome until those of the personal kind are encountered and dissolved, and this has to be done consciously.

It has already been stated that time is a factor in the soul's bondage. It must now become an aid towards freedom. Expanding the mind to know *Brahman* will entail placing it upon *Brahman* more and more of the time; this is actually the opposite of obsessing with the world, and with matter. Placing the one before the zeros was Sri Ramakrishna's way of describing this process. Since matter has no consciousness of its own, being much like the moon shining by borrowed light from the sun, focusing on it only leads back to it. As he quipped, the dinosaurs obsessed with matter, and they actually turned into it, i.e., stone. Even the very mind that focuses on matter is a type of subtle matter. It, with its ego concomitant, are also zeros in the end; they disappear, inexplicably and unaccountably, in deep sleep, what to speak of at the time of death (we are to contemplate this as the dull light of the mind/soul seeking heaven, rather than formless bliss).

Thus, placing the mind on *Brahman* begins to dissolve its past impressions around and about matter (the five Great Elements, *Panchamahabhutas*), and *maya* (the cosmic illusion). The mind is subtle matter, and with its inherent abilities, projects gross matter. Therefore, if the mind is to study matter at all, it must do so from a safe distance. All studies that involve the five elements, then, undertaken in scientific fashion, are to be seen as studying the mind's own projections. The false premise that beings were born in nature has to be disproven for the falsely thinking man of today, for all of nature has come forth from the mind. As for the Soul, it cannot be created or projected. It is "acreate;" it has no birth and death. It is originless. That Soul is *Brahman*.

The closest that the thinking mind can come to Divine Reality without dissolving into its own essence is to meditate upon *Ishvara*. The *Ishtam*, the Divine Ideal, is the highest concept of Reality that the human being can envision, said Swami Vivekananda. He also stated that beings on earth must have such an ideal, for here the Truth of *Brahman* is duly veiled from sight.

The Father of *Yoga* (*Raja Yoga*, *Patanjala*) has gone to such extent as to call *Ishvara* "A special kind of being distinct from man, in-so-much as He is not subject to ignorance and the products of ignorance." He also reveals that "*Ishvara* is the most unique Being in existence," and that "*Yoga* is more easily attained if worship of *Ishvara* is adhered to." In other words, "God with form (*Ishvara*) is a unique Soul who is never tainted by activity or its various potentialities." *Klesha-karma-vipakashayair a-para-mrshtah purusha-vishesha ishvarah.* (*klesha*, obstacle; *karma*, activity; *vipaka*, development; *ashayaih*, potentialities; *apara-mrshtah*, not tainted; *purusha-visheshah*, unique soul; *ishvarah*; God with attributes).

"What people worship here," then, as the *Katha Upanisad* repeats over and over again in its *slokas*, is matter, or objects, or egos; they do not worship God/*Brahman*, as *Brahman* is none of those things. The *Svetashvatara Upanisad* states unequivocally, that *Brahman* is not matter, energy, or thought, so the seeker of Wisdom is to look beyond those three worldly shrines and find the Temple of Truth. *Ishvara* stands as the Eternal Gateway between the highest level of form and pure Formlessness itself. Contemplating It will awaken divine memory in the soul, then,

The Fivefold Strata of Sacrifice

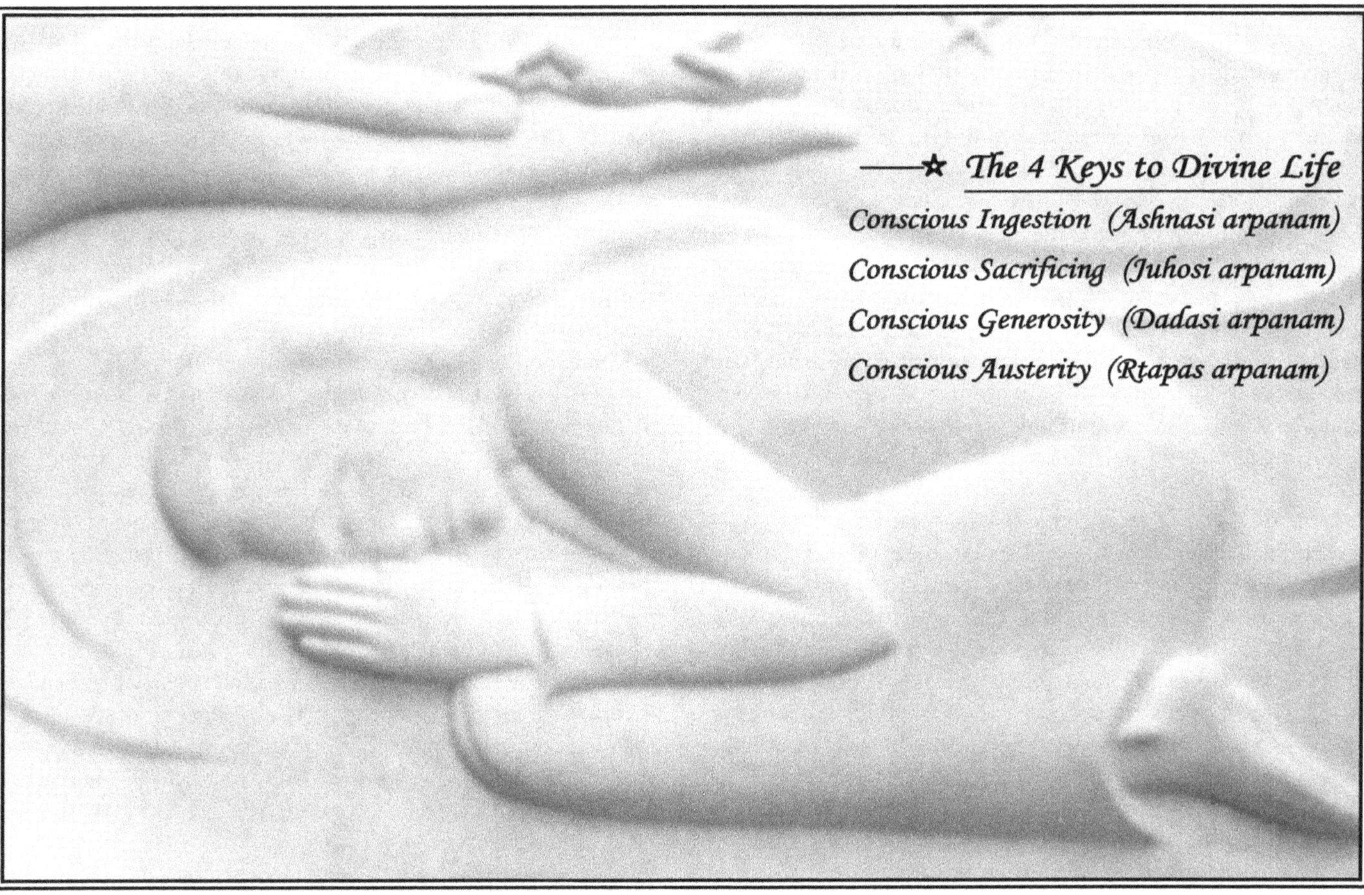

> ★ **The 4 Keys to Divine Life**
> *Conscious Ingestion (Ashnasi arpanam)*
> *Conscious Sacrificing (Juhosi arpanam)*
> *Conscious Generosity (Dadasi arpanam)*
> *Conscious Austerity (Rtapas arpanam)*

Deva Yajna

"The miserly do not come to this world of the gods, and the foolish do not praise them. Only the one of good character, who takes pleasure in giving, becomes happy in that realm." — Lord Buddha

Rishi Yajna

"He who with supreme devotion to Me will teach this profound philosophy to My devotees, shall doubtless come to Me alone. Nor is there any among men who renders dearer service to Me than he." — Sri Krishna

Pitri Yajna

"The knowers of the three Vedas, worshipping Me by sacrifices, pray for the way to heaven. They reach the holy world of the Lord of the Devas and enjoy it in the celestial planes of the Devas. Having enjoyed the vast world of heaven, they return to the world of mortals on the exhaustion of their merits. Thus abiding by the injunctions of the Vedas, desiring objects of desire, they go and they come." — Sri Krishna

Nara Yajna

"Down on your face before Him, and make a great sacrifice; the sacrifice of a whole life for humanity, for whom He comes from time to time, whom he loves above all — the poor, the lowly, the oppressed." — Swami Vivekananda

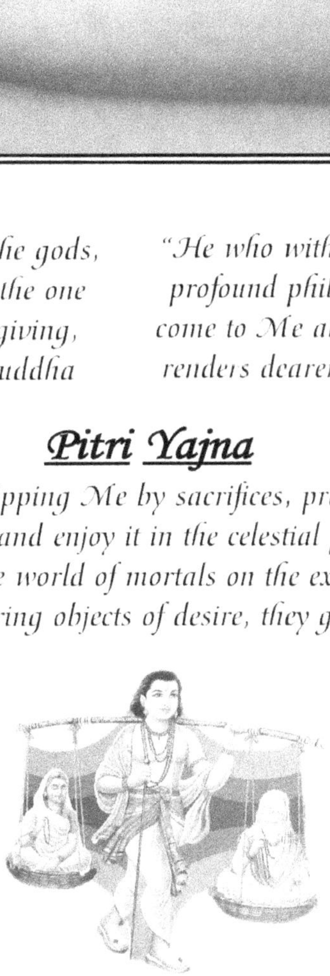

Bhuta Yajna

"That one who takes good and shuns evil, acting as if holding a pair of scales, is indeed wise. By nonviolence to all living beings, even to animals, one becomes noble." — Lord Buddha

Chart by Babaji Bob Kindler
Sculpture by Eli Marozzi

Property of SRV Associations

and cause it to recall the primal awareness of timeless, spaceless, Transcendental Consciousness.

Short of this more direct route to divine recollection, study of the scriptures is recommended. Called *svadhyaya* in Yoga, its singular aim is reached by *shruti* (hearing the nondual texts), *yukti* (analyzing and contemplating them), and *anubhava* (gaining direct experience from what they relate) according to the Vedanta. Many convincing reasons are given to set the student on this swift and ignorance-destroying pathway (*jnana yoga*), but the most evident, though secret (hidden) one is the existence of the subtle power in words themselves. Every letter of a meaningful word is impregnated with *Shakti* power, so contemplating an entire sentence (*sloka, sutra, sura, mantra*) will confer immense force for realization. A seeker on the path of divine remembrance only needs to encounter a special soul who has awakened via the vehicle of powerful words, and receive a transmission from him/her.

To aid in this endeavor, the seeker should practice either moderation or outright celibacy. Just as keeping one's appetite for food under control saves energy and keeps the organs healthier, so too does saving the subtle physical and sexual energy from expenditure aid in building up power for retentive memory. Most elderly people are seen to be devoid of both intelligence and memory towards the end of their lives, while beings who have practiced spiritual disciplines from their early life have full access to wisdom. Frittering away sexual energy early on, and engaging in mindless actions for the sake of mundane pleasures, are two surefire ways of courting forgetfulness of everything that otherwise may have conferred sharp remembrance and profound insight on the embodied soul. To conclude on this point, dire *vismriti* is waiting to veil, then rob, the mind of its innate abilities when the subtle shield of continence is compromised via careless and unadvised promiscuity.

All of the above also pertains to those who use intoxicants, imagining them to be helpful for spiritual life. They are detrimental, particularly in the long run, and obviously, the memory gets fogged over by their use. The soul only enters its next life addicted to them, which is seen in today's societies and their peoples.

The blessing of *mantra-diksha* is taken up next. No doubt that it is a splendid tool to utilize for keeping the memory of spiritual principles forefront in the mind. But in this day and age, particularly in the West, this type of special initiation is accepted by a cross-section of souls, who then engage in it for a few weeks, or months, and give it up. One soul on record took initiation from Sri Sarada Devi on one occasion, then came back a few days later and complained to Her that the *mantra* did not work! "No, no, my son," She responded: "*You have to repeat it day and night, for some time. Go and do this for Me, then return. If then you still have not made any progress, I will help you.*" If the Mother of the Universe, Herself, gives a *mantra*, and people do not take it seriously, then how much more will be the impediments in the way of those who receive the *mantra* from a *mantri guru*?

And further, as the chart implies, the constant attendance upon the *guru*, and upon other forms of holy company, must accompany the recitation of the *mantra*, for the *mantra* will bring up hidden obstacles, and this process is best encountered in holy company, not on one's own, without a guide. And so, the wise student finds a good path, fortuitously meets the *guru*, takes initiation, then remains close at hand while *sadhana* is accomplished over phases of time. Even sharing experiences after spiritual awakening has occurred is best to do with the *guru*; one refrains from burning bridges in the *Guru/Shishya* relationship in India. And relative to these points, as the penultimate teaching on the chart relates, *japa* itself burns obstacles when it becomes mature as a practice. At first it protects the mind as it engages in *sadhana*, for facets of *maya* (family, ancestors, past *karmas*) will naturally close in on the soul, leaving it temporarily defenseless while it orients itself to the new regimen. But once the *mantra* penetrates into the unconscious layers of the mind, it becomes a means to attaining spiritual power. Soon thereafter it transforms into a "*bubbling spring of ambrosia,*" as the scriptures relate, leaving behind an eternal smile on the features of the now, free soul.

The final aid in recovering one's memory of the Divine and its superlative qualities comes in the form of ongoing *yajna*, or religious sacrifice. This is a "natural part of everyday life" type of practice. Sacrifices to the gods, the *rishis*, the ancestors, the humans, and the subhuman species are all included and enjoined. It stands to reason that, when human beings are not occupying the physical body, and are in the bardo of disembodiment or subtle embodiment, they, too, inhabit the forms of any of these groups. Therefore, worshipping them here on earth, while embodied, brings back memories of periods of time spent with them. In accord with the subject of this article, this is one of the methods that can be used to ignite and bring forth subtle memory. *Yajna* has other benefits as well, which help spiritualize life and actions and remove defects from the mind. The chart on the previous page reveals the art of *yajna*.

The main chart we have studied shows the earth plane as well as the fourth world, and reveals what can stand as veiling potential between communing with them. It would be a grave mistake to think that the inner worlds are in outer space; only more of the outer world/universe is out there. Beings get to and from the inner worlds (at the time of birth and death), from gross, to subtle, to causal, via *nadis*, which are hidden nerve channels in the mind (not the brain) running throughout the 7 *lokas*, or seven *chakras*. It would also be a misrepresentation to talk of these *nadis* as being in the physical body; only physical versions of the subtle nadis are there. Everything on earth is a mere reflection of what is internal. The *Upanisads* state:

Purnamadah purnamidam purnat purnamudachyate
Purnasya purnamadaya purnameva vasishyate

What is infinite, within, is Eternal; what is finite, though external, is also infinite. From the Infinite the finite has come, but being Infinite, only Infinite remains. Aum Peace, Peace, Peace

Babaji Bob Kindler, initiated disciple of Swami Aseshanandaji Maharaj, is the Spiritual Director of the SRV Associations with its two centers in Hawaii and Oregon. A teacher of religion and spirituality and a prolific author, his books include The Avadhut, Twenty-Four Aspects of Mother Kali, Ten Divine Articles of Sri Durga, Swami Vivekananda Vijnanagita, Sri Sarada Vijnanagita, An Extensive Anthology of Sri Ramakrishna's Stories, A Quintessential Yoga Vasishtha, Reclaiming Kundalini Yoga, Cosmic Quintuplications, Jnana Matra, Manasana, Footfalls of the Indian Rishis, and others. Founder and Artistic Director of Jai Ma Music, he is also an accomplished musician, recording artist, and composer, who has produced over twenty-five albums of instrumental and devotional music.

VEDANTA 101
Triple Teachings for Peace & Transcendence

Vedanta and Patanjala Yoga offer plentiful teachings and instructions for the *sadhaka*. In daily life, it can be helpful to have a simple teaching, backed by the philosophical systems and lives of illumined beings, to alert us when thoughts and actions run counter to spiritual teachings and Truth. Rather than a point of dogma, this discerning move leads to real happiness and peace by training the mind to serve us instead of tyrannize us with bad moods, unworthy actions, and complicated karmas. The first two teachings on the forthcoming page are imminently practical: The Three Stages of the Mind's Evolution and the Three Obstacles to Self-Realization. The final one shows us the stages we should expect to experience if we take spiritual life seriously.

The Three Stages of the Mind's Evolution

"Brooding Mind, Thinking Mind, and Illumined Mind" describes the mind in ways we can all relate to, and which we see around us in others constantly, from our children and relatives, to coworkers, to media personalities. This teaching is more than recognizing how the *guna* of *tamas* in the mind makes one lethargic, which can be overcome by *rajas*, desire-based actions, and lead to temporary calmness, *sattva*. Mere recognition of these three qualities of the mind and managing them with pleasurable diversions only results in cycling back to *rajas* and *tamas* because spiritual truths and practices were not applied. In contrast, this triple teaching (*triputi*) is intended to break the cycle permanently. Brooding mind, in essence, is keeping one's mind fixed on passing phenomena via attachment and aversion and leaves no room for higher thought. Thinking mind is engaging the intellect in spiritual teachings and applying them. To give one example: one notices the mind brooding with fear and anxiety over an illness. Recognition of the state of "brooding mind" can be used as a trigger to remember spiritual teachings and apply them, such as discrimination between the Self and the body, or teachings concerning forbearance, indifference, or simply placing the mind on thoughts of God and spiritual Truth. In *Yoga*, this would be called shifting from pain-bearing thoughts to non-pain-bearing thoughts (*klishta* to *aklishta*). Another example is noticing the mind brooding on anticipated pleasures, fantasizing over future enjoyments, or simply living a day-to-day life devoid of spiritual practice. The ability to take one's mind off of phenomena is strengthened by this practice of placing the mind on wisdom and leads the mind back to "its original state of blissful, equanimous Awareness."

The Three Obstacles to Self-Realization

Sri Ramakrishna would often say, "All troubles will cease when the ego dies." He himself knew the freedom and bliss of merging the individual self into the One without a Second. Upon returning to relative consciousness, he then used the "ripe ego" to navigate in the world. The three main ways the ego asserts itself is, at its root, the sense of separation from all else - God, beings, and nature. This error arises from *avidya* (root ignorance), or *maya*, which makes indivisible Reality appear divided and veils one's identity as that Reality. This sense of separation gives rise to the sense of ownership: my body, my relatives, my possessions, my knowledge, which cause attachment, aversion, pride, jealousy, and other unsavory passions to flourish. It also gives rise to the sense of doership, or agency. Thus, Sri Ramakrishna would instruct seekers, "*...only an ignorant person feels that he is the doer. A man verily becomes liberated in life if he feels: 'God is the Doer. He alone is doing everything. I am doing nothing.' Man's sufferings and worries spring only from his persistent thought that he is the doer.*" (*Gospel of Sri Ramakrishna*, p. 152) Since God alone exists, then the sense of separation, ownership, and agency are an incorrect reading of Reality. We can easily train ourselves to recognize these three obstacles to Self-Realization in our day-to-day life, and shift our thinking accordingly. This can begin with seeing oneself as a custodian rather than an owner, and assume the mental position that God is the owner of the universe. Instead of being the agent of action and taking pride (or its opposite) in results, one works as a servant of God and offers up the results. This ripens the ego. Instead of constantly affirming one's individuality and therefore one's separation from God, one seeks to remember constantly that *Brahman* and *Atman* (apparently individual Self) are one, or that God is the whole and one is part of that Divine Being. This is facilitated via formal contemplation of this truth.

The Three Plateaus of Spiritual Evolution

This final *triputi* serves as a road map for the spiritual journey. The first plateau, or stage, is *shuddhi*, purification. In the context of *Yoga* this means practicing the *yamas* (nonviolence, truthfulness, non-stealing, moderation, non-acquisitiveness), which saves us from creating new negative *karmas*. The deeper purification begins when study of revealed scriptures with a guru, austerity, self-surrender to God/*Ishvara*, and other disciplines are practiced. This purification prepares the mind to be able to assimilate spiritual teachings and engage wholeheartedly in *Yoga Sadhana*, spiritual practices that transform the subtle mental *samskaras*, the inherent tendencies lodged in the unconscious mind. With the practice of well-guided meditation, the five *kleshas*, as listed in the accompanying quote on the chart, "ignorance, egotism, attachment, aversion, fear of death," are rendered less and less troublesome and finally reduced to the state of burnt ropes that cannot bind.

In *Footfalls of the Indian Rishis*, the author, Babaji Bob Kindler, points out how the Three Plateaus of Spiritual Evolution mirror and work together with the first two *triputis*. "*...when the mind is under the influence of the tendency to brood, and struggling with a false sense of ownership, it needs the power of purification to place things into proper perspective. And when thinking mind and its cohort called the sense of agency start up, yoga-sadhana, the power of transformation, becomes a valuable spiritual asset. And finally, when illumined mind becomes the norm, and the final sense of separation between the soul and nature and the Soul and Reality comes up, the ability for complete transcendence of even the subtlest pairs of opposites via the mind's well-honed discrimination arises.*" (p.220)

The Three Stages of Mind's Evolution
The Three Plateaus of Spiritual Evolution
The Three Obstacles to Self-Realization

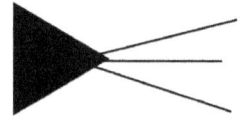 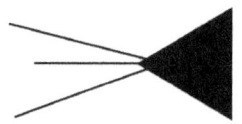

The 3 Stages of Mind's Evolution

Chitta-Chinta — Brooding Mind   **Chitta-Lochana — Thinking Mind**

Chitta-Bhati — Illumined Mind

"Overcoming the mind's tendency to brood by utilizing its inherent powers of thoughtful insight augers a sure sign of spiritual evolution. Within the still and peaceful atmosphere of wisdom samadhi that results, the mind gets transported back to its original state of blissful and equanimous Awareness." — Babaji Bob Kindler

The Three Obstacles — To Self-Realization

Ahamta Mamata — Sense of Ownership

"I am the doer, my actions are important, I do good to others... these are signs of the unripe ego."

Kartrtya — Sense of Agency

"Pride in one's wealth, in one's learning, and in one's possessions leave a stain on the mind."

Vibhaga — Sense of Separation

"Prahlada had two moods. Sometimes he would feel that he was God. In that mood he would say, 'Thou art verily I.' But when he was conscious of his ego, he looked upon God as his master and himself as the servant." — Sri Ramakrishna

Vighna ... *Vinashana*

The 3 Plateaus of Spiritual Evolution

1. Shuddhi — Purification

"Ascetic observances, silent recitation, study of scriptures, reciting the mantra, surrender of all practices to God under the auspice of devotion — this is authentic purification."

2. Yoga-Sadhana — Transformation

"Ignorance, egotism, attachment, aversion, fear of death — afflictions like these are to be made progressively more and more subtle — reduced, and finally eliminated via meditation."

3. Viveka-jnana — Transcendence

"The unwavering illumination of discriminatory wisdom is the way to transcendence." — Lord Patanjali

Chart by Babaji Bob Kindler

Property of SRV Associations

THE BLOSSOMING OF CONSCIOUSNESS
As Seen In Sri Ramakrishna

In recent times, the study of consciousness has caught the attention of a great many western philosophers and psychologists, even though the Indian and Western concepts of consciousness are vastly different. In Indian tradition, consciousness is the essence of the Supreme Reality and is called *chit* or *chid*, whereas in Western tradition, consciousness is considered a function of the mind, which in Indian tradition is called *chitta*, because it is through mind that the *chit* manifests itself. This relation between *chitta* and *chit* is very important for understanding the unfoldment of consciousness. Since *chit* manifests through *chitta*, modifications of *chitta* and the states of *chitta* are of prime importance in understanding the unfoldment of consciousness.

What are the normal states of consciousness in us according to Indian thought? They are waking (*jâgrata*), dreaming (*svapna*) and deep-sleep (*sushupti*) consciousness. According to the Indian tradition, there is another state, called *turiya*, or transcendental, in which consciousness functions or manifests itself, more or less bereft of the limitations of mind or *chitta*. By the practice of *yoga*, one can transcend the three normal states of consciousness and enter into transcendental consciousness. Some people have coined the word 'yogic consciousness' for that state, and there could be various types of such *yogic* consciousness. Sri Ramakrishna's life is like a large museum of this *yogic* consciousness, and we can now study that rich museum.

Various States of Consciousness in Sri Ramakrishna

It will be helpful to trace the changes in consciousness as they occurred in Sri Ramakrishna. It is on record that Sri Ramakrishna had, on several occasions in childhood, showed signs of altered consciousness. Once, while playing the part of Shiva in a drama, he manifested Shiva consciousness and became still in a trance-like state, called *samâdhi*. On another occasion he was so stunned by the beauty of a row of white cranes flying in front of a dark rain cloud, that he lost all outer consciousness. He was neither awake, nor dreaming, nor asleep. For all practical purposes, he fell "unconscious" to the onlookers. But later, while describing the experience, he said that he was experiencing great bliss.

These events were spontaneous, and no apparent cause could be ascribed to them except that Sri Ramakrishna was temperamentally more prone to such events. But, let us now turn to the period when he consciously and deliberately undertook *yogic* practices, or spiritual practices. The practices were intense and serious, but we need not go into all their details.

The first thing to note was that he almost completely conquered dream and sleep states of consciousness. He did not sleep for six long years. The second result was that his nervous system and physiology changed due to the impact of *sâdhanâ*. He consciously practiced renunciation of money, and the result was he could not touch coins, or even metal, even in his sleep. His limbs would recoil if they even accidently touched a coin. The third result was, that at the height of spiritual yearning, he had the vision of God.

From the point of unfoldment of consciousness, his description of that vision is significant:

"It was as if the houses, doors, temples, and all other things vanished altogether; as if there was nothing anywhere! And what I saw was a boundless, infinite conscious Sea of Light!" The Master told the devotees that at that time he saw *"a luminous sea of Consciousness."*

But what about the Divine Mother's form consisting of pure Consciousness only – the form of Hers with hands that give boons and freedom from fear? Did the Master have the vision of that form as well in that sea of Light? It appears that he did; for as soon as he regained the slightest outward consciousness at the time of that vision he, we are told, uttered repeatedly the word "Mother" in a voice choked with emotion.

Sri Ramakrishna did not stop efforts after this one superconscious experience. He went on with his *yogic sâdhanâ* till that state of consciousness became natural to him. He started virtually living in that superconscious state. The divine consciousness became more real to him than even the waking consciousness. He expressed this truth in answer to Swami Vivekananda's question, "Sir, have you seen God?" in the following words: "Yes, I have seen God. I have seen Him more tangibly than I am talking to you at this moment."

After this, Sri Ramakrishna lived at various levels of consciousness – often at the normal consciousness like any other individual, having waking, dream, and deep sleep experiences. However, there was a vast difference between his waking state and that of ordinary individuals. Even in the normal waking state, divine consciousness was very much present in him. Only a fraction of his mind, say 25%, was active in waking state, whereas 75% of his mind used to remain merged in divine consciousness. This state of consciousness has been recommended by Swami Vivekananda also, when he advised us to keep 75% of our minds in God and work with 25% in the world. Sri Ramakrishna used to advise catching hold of God with one hand and doing the worldly duties with the other hand, meaning thereby, to keep a part of the mind always in divine consciousness.

Secondly, there was that state in which he saw God everywhere, in which the forms of external objects of the world were also visible. He expressed this, saying, "*I am seeing everything made of God, as it were.*" He could experience the two states of consciousness simultaneously. Then, there were times when he would lose all outward consciousness and merge completely into divine consciousness. He would then totally lose all outer (waking) consciousness. Many times he tried to describe this state, but failed, the reason being that during that state, the mind itself gets transcended. This is called *nirvikalpa samâdhi*, and the *Vedas* also verify it as a state beyond mind, which cannot be described in words: *Yato vâcho nivartante, aprâpya manasâ saha* (Taittriyopanishad).

The various levels of superconscious states in which Sri Ramakrishna normally and naturally lived can be best described in the words of Swami Vivekananda, to whom he actually transmitted these states. Sri Ramakrishna touched Swami Vivekananda, Narendra, twice. Once, during their first meeting, everything that formed the content of Naren's waking consciousness, started dissolving, until finally, his ego also began to disappear. Later, Narendra, then Swami Vivekananda, described this as follows:

'*His touch at once gave rise to a novel experience within me. With my eyes open I saw that the walls, and everything in the room, whirled rapidly and vanished into naught, and the whole universe together with my individuality was about to merge in an all-encompassing mysterious void! I was terribly frightened and thought that I was facing death, for the loss of individuality meant nothing short of that to me at that time. Unable to control myself I cried out, 'What is it that you are doing to me! I have my parents at home!' He laughed aloud at this and, stroking my chest, said: 'All right, let it rest now. Everything will come in time!' The wonder of it was that no sooner had he said this than that strange experience of mine vanished.*"

On the Second Occasion

"*That magic touch of the Master on that day immediately brought a wonderful change over my mind. I was astounded to find that, really, there was nothing in the universe but God! I saw this quite clearly, but kept silent to see whether the impression would last. But it did not abate in the course of the entire day. Whether eating, or lying down, or going to college, I had the same experience, and felt myself always in a sort of trance. When there came a slight change in this state, the world began to appear dream-like. While walking in Cornwallis Square, I would strike my head against the iron railings to see if they were real, or only a dream. This state of things continued for some days. When I became normal again, I realized that I must have had a glimpse of the Advaita state.*"

Swami Vivekananda has also compared such states of consciousness with the experience of seeing a mirage. That is, one may be deceived by a mirage to begin with, but once it is understood one may still continue to see it but will not be deceived by it. Similarly, after a spiritual experience, one continues to see the world but knows that it is unreal, like a mirage.

To recapitulate then, Sri Ramakrishna naturally dwelt in three types of superconscious states:

1. When he totally transcended the relative world and merged into transcendental consciousness of Brahman.
2. When he saw the world as God.
3. When he experienced the waking state as unreal, as if in a dream, like the dream state or like a mirage.

The first state cannot be described in words, except by negation i.e., "*Not this, not this*" (neti neti). In the second, the phenomenal world is seen as God, and in the third, the phenomenal world appears, unreal or shadowy, like a dream.

The Uniqueness of Bhava Mukha

Apart from these three superconscious states, Sri Ramakrishna also dwelt in one more state called *bhâva-mukha*. The word *bhâva* means idea or mood, or mental states of the modifications of chitta, and *mukha* means gateway, the mouth, or the opening to or the beginning of ideas. Thus, *bhâva-mukha* means the state of consciousness from where moods or mental modifications arise.

Soon after the attainment of the *advaitic* consciousness (*nirvikalpa samâdhi*) in which Sri Ramakrishna remained for almost four months at a stretch, he received a divine command: "*Remain in bhâva-mukha.*" In other words, he was commanded not to get merged in nondual consciousness, nor yet remain totally at the level of mental modifications where most of us normally live, but instead to remain at the borderline of these two realms, i.e., at the state of consciousness where all the various moods and ideas and mental modifications arise. In philosophical terms, he was commanded, and accordingly lived for the rest of his life, at the borderline between the absolute and the relative, between transcendental consciousness and manifest consciousness. This was the reason why he could, with ease, access and know the moods of all the various people who came to him, or whom he met. He could read the minds of people just as one sees into an almirah through its glass panel. What a remarkable state of consciousness!

Practice of Yoga

We have discussed the various states of consciousness, *chit*, in Sri Ramakrishna. Let us now turn to *chitta*, the mind, through which *chit* manifests, of Sri Ramakrishna. For all practical purposes, consciousness as we understand it today, refers mainly to mind or *chitta*.

Through spiritual practice, Sri Ramakrishna had totally transformed his mind, *chitta*. Patanjali, the father of the *Yoga* system, has defined *Yoga* as "*control of thought waves.*" This again is of two types. In one, all thought waves, except one, are controlled, whereas in the other, all thought waves are controlled. The first is called *savikalpa samâdhi*, the other is called *nirvikalpa samâdhi*. *Savikalpa samâdhi*, in which there is some content, or *pratyaya*, in the consciousness, is again of various types. And interestingly, in Sri Ramakrishna, most of these, are seen.

Take for example, his merging into *samâdhi* while explaining the precepts of the *Vaishnava* cult. While elaborating the precept that one must have compassion on creatures, he went into *samâdhi*, and on returning to normal consciousness, threw such an extraordinary light of wisdom on this precept, that it turned out to become the guiding principle of the future Ramakrishna Mission. He said that man was too weak and helpless to have compassion on creatures. Instead, one must serve creatures considering them as gods. This *samâdhi*, according to Patanjali's *Yoga Sutras*, is called *savichâra samâdhi*, in which intense concentration is applied on a particular precept.

In *nirvikalpa samâdhi*, his mind became one, as it were, with absolute transcendental consciousness. Not only his mind stopped working, even the bodily functions came to a standstill. The corneal reflex (the blinking of the eyelids if something touches the surface of the eyeball) was lost, and the pulse could not be felt. Even the heart stopped beating!!

In the *savikalpa samâdhi*, Sri Ramakrishna had various *bhâvas* — heightened spiritual moods or emotions — and "visions" — both visual and auditory — depending upon the idea or object occupying his mind or totally coloring his mind. For example, when the thought or image of Rama or Krishna completely occupied his *chitta*, and his consciousness was fully possessed by the idea, he had the vision of Rama or Krishna. Such visions of Sri Ramakrishna are innumerable. At times, this coloring of his mind or *chitta* would be so deep, that he would loose his separate identity, and become, at it were, one with the object of meditation, and he acted and behaved in a manner much different from his natural way. While practicing the mood of a *Gopi*, a woman worshipper and lover of Sri Krishna, he thought and even physically acted like a woman.

In the path of *Bhakti* or devotion, love of God is cultivated and heightened. This leads to changes in consciousness, mostly related to emotions like extreme agony at the separation from God and intense joy at the experience of union. It is said in devotional texts that there are as many as sixteen varieties of spiritual emotional moods. All of these were experienced by Sri Ramakrishna. Sometimes he would feel intense agony, which even manifested at the physical level as burning sensation in the body, excessive perspiration, horripilation, tremors, etc. At the other extreme, he would sing and dance in great joy.

According to *Yoga*, mind is all-pervasive. There is an ocean of *chitta*, or mind, and all the minds are interconnected. This is called *chittâkâsha*, or the "sky of mind!" This also implies that with proper *yogic* training, a person can communicate with other minds, can know their thoughts and feelings, and even control or modify them. Sri Ramakrishna had that capacity. His consciousness had expanded to encompass all living creatures. He would feel pain when someone stepped on the grass of the lawn. He would, during one stage, avoid stepping on grass while walking, since he actually saw consciousness in the blades of grass. Likewise once, while watching one boatman strike another with a rod, Sri Ramakrishna cried out in pain and the mark of the rod was seen on his back.

To be able to discern the ideas and thoughts arising in other minds was a daily affair with Sri Ramakrishna. Many people have recorded that if ever they went to Sri Ramakrishna with any specific question in their minds, they were often surprised to find that he would start talking about the same subjects which were uppermost in their minds.

Conclusion

The amazing unfoldment of consciousness as seen in Sri Ramakrishna, in its variety and extent, is unprecedented in the spiritual history of the world. He continuously lived at an entirely different level of consciousness than that of others. This he attained by intense spiritual practice. These practices encompass a

> "The various levels of superconscious states in which Sri Ramakrishna normally and naturally lived can be best described in the words of Swami Vivekananda, to whom he actually transmitted these states. Sri Ramakrishna touched Swami Vivekananda, Narendra, twice. Once, during their first meeting, everything that formed the content of Naren's waking consciousness, started dissolving, until finally, his ego also began to disappear."

wide range, and with each type of spiritual practice, there were corresponding changes in consciousness. He never theorized about these matters. He was simply content to live the life. And this is the great lesson for all of us. It is far more important for us to do spiritual practice and actually experience altered states of consciousness, rather than merely speculate about them.

A former editor of the Vedanta Keshari, and previously of the Ramakrishna Mission Home of Service, Swami Brameshananda is a senior monk of the Ramakrishna Order and until recently was the Secretary of the Ramakrishna Mission Ashram in Chandigarh, India. Over the years his writings in Hindi and English have appeared in several journals, including Prabuddha Bharata, Vedanta Keshari, and Nectar of Nondual Truth. He specializes in themes related to Jainism. He is now retired and is living an inner, contemplative life in Varanasi.

Wisdom Facets From the Gem of Truth

Sri Ramakrishna

Holy Mother, Sri Sarada Devi

"To the Formless Brahman via the Ishvara Form"

"Some reach the formless God by worshipping God with form, and again some attain God with form by adopting the sadhana of the formless God. The formless aspect is of two kinds: mature and immature. The mature one is very high indeed and must be reached through God with form. The immature one, as professed by the Brahmos, is like darkness perceived merely by closing the eyes."

(The Gospel of Sri Ramakrishna)

Devotion to Duality

"Duality is meant for ordinary human beings who are attached to sense objects. An excellent practice for them is to chant the Lord's name loudly according to the Narada Pancharatra."

(Ramakrishna & His Divine Play)

Families Come and Go

"Is there no hope for householders? Certainly there is. They must practice spiritual discipline in solitude for some days. Thus they will acquire knowledge and devotion. Then it will not hurt them to lead the life of the world. But when you practice discipline in solitude, keep yourself entirely away from your family."

(The Gospel of Sri Ramakrishna)

Discrimination Loves Compassion

"Well, is it an easy matter to realize that lust and gold are truly unreal and to have the firm conviction that the world does not exist, and has never existed? Is it possible to achieve this without God's compassion? This [realization] happens only if God graciously bestows that conviction on a person. Otherwise, can anyone achieve this through self-effort? A human being is after all a tiny creature with very limited powers. How much effort can an individual exert with such meager strength?"

(The Gospel of Sri Ramakrishna)

Bringing Her Out From Hiding

"It is the Master who taught the name of Mother. Did people know before that God is Mother? It is Her creation. She gives birth to all beings and again swallows them. To swallow means to give liberation. It is all Her sport, Her play."

(The Compassionate Mother)

You Get To The Father Through The Mother

"Do not fear, my child. Always remember that the Master is behind you. I am also with you. As long as you remember me, your mother, why should you be frightened? The Master said to me, 'At the end of their life, I shall certainly liberate those who come to you.'"

(Sri Sarada Devi & Her Divine Play)

How to Undo The Mystery of Maya

"This body has a form, but the mind is boundless. It can be expanded like the vast space, but it is bound by maya. People do not know this mystery of maya, so they suffer and inflict suffering on others."

(Sri Sarada Devi & Her Divine Play)

How To Achieve Wetness Consciousness

"How can the Master's service be dry? You should reflect upon the cause of dryness. The human mind becomes accustomed to a certain condition, and when it goes to another situation, it feels uncomfortable and it longs for the previous condition. At that time one should pray to the Master. You will see that he will make your mind joyful."

(Sri Sarada Devi & Her Divine Play)

From Loneliness To The Alone

"Our Master alone is Maheshwara, as well as Maheshwari. He alone is the embodiment of all the deities. He alone is the embodiment of all mystic syllables. Through him alone one can worship all gods and goddesses."

(Compassionate Mother)

Wisdom Facets From the Gem of Truth

Swami Vivekananda   Disciples & Devotees of Sri Ramakrishna

The Two Wings of the Bird are Nondifferent
"The realization of Divine Love comes to none unless they be a perfect Jnani. Does not Vedanta say that Brahman is Sat-Chitananda? There is no controversy between the Jnani and Bhakta regarding the Sat aspect of Brahman. Only the Jnanis lay greater stress on His aspect as Chit, or knowledge, while the Bhaktas keep the aspect of Ananda, or love, more in view. But no sooner is the essence of Chit realized then the essence of Ananda is also realized."

(Talks with Swami Vivekananda)

Go To Ramakrishna
"Everyone who has gone to Sri Ramakrishna has advanced in spirituality, is advancing in spirituality and will advance. One spray from the ocean of His spirituality, if realized, will make gods of men. Such a synthesis of universal ideas you will never find in the history of the world again. He Himself is his own parallel; has He any exemplar?"

(Talks With Swami Vivekananda)

Brahman: The Only Wonder of the World
"There is nothing wonderful in this universe. Ignorance constitutes the only darkness, which covers all things and makes them look mysterious. When everything is lighted by knowledge, the sense of mystery vanishes from the face of things. Even such an inscrutable thing as Maya, which brings the most impossible things to pass, disappears. So know Him; by knowing Him everything else is known."

(Talks With Swami Vivekananda)

Triple Gift for Qualification
"First of all comes the gift of food; next comes the gift of learning, and highest of all is the gift of knowledge. We must harmonize all three to produce aspirants who are prepared."

(Talks with Swami Vivekananda)

Divine Work First
"Without doing japa and meditation it is not possible to work according to the ideals shown by the Master and Swamiji. Only after the mind is purified by spiritual practices can one work in the proper spirit, and not before. It is not at all proper to slacken our spiritual practices just because we are engaged in some kind of work."

(Swami Brahmananda, The Eternal Companion)

He Did the Universal Kundalini
"Swamiji has stated that the Satya Yuga has commenced with the Master's birth. The Master has demonstrated by his life and sadhana that we are all children of the same God. He has awakened the primordial power, Shakti, which he would address as 'Mother'. At Dakshineshwar, the Master would fan Mother Kali while singing the song 'Awake, O Mother Kulakundalini!' He did not, however, do this, to awaken his own Kundalini; that was already awakened. Swamiji has said that the Master has awakened the Universal Kundalini. This will lead to the manifestation of virtuous qualities in human beings throughout the world. All the religions of the world will be rejuvenated, and the whole world will be blessed."

(Swami Sivananda, In The Divine Realm)

No Time for God?
"The Master's grace and His blessings are not lacking. But how many are there who set their sail to catch His breeze of grace? How many bend their heads to receive His blessings? People's minds are busy with trivial things. Who wants the real treasure? They talk big, but they don't strive to earn anything. They want to get everything without effort. People can manage to do all kinds of worldly work, but when it comes to keeping recollectedness of God they ask: 'But where is the time to do it?'"

(Swami Brahmananda, In The Divine Realm)

SCRIPTURAL SAYINGS
of the World's Religious Traditions

"An anthill increases by accumulation. Medicine is consumed by distribution. That which is feared lessens by association. These are things to understand. Yet, he who knoweth such precepts by heart, but faileth to practice them, is like unto one who lighteth a lamp and then shutteth his eyes."

"The disciples came and asked, 'Why do you speak to the people in parables?' He replied, 'Because the knowledge of the secrets of the kingdom of heaven have been given to you, but not to them. This is why I speak to them in parables. Though seeing, they do not see, though hearing, they do not hear. People's hearts have become calloused, Otherwise they might see with their eyes, hear with their ears, understand with their hearts, and I would heal them. But blessed are your eyes because they see, and your ears because they hear it.'"

"And Paradise will be brought near to the righteous, not far off. And it will be said to them, 'This is what you were promised, for whoever constantly turned to Allah and kept up His commandments, who were in awe of the Most Compassionate without seeing Him, have come with a heart turning only to Him. Enter it in peace. This is the Day of eternal life!'"

"When ignorance is dispelled there is neither day nor night, neither being nor nonbeing. There is only that Auspicious One who is imperishable, and Who is worthy of being worshipped by the creator. From that One has proceeded the ancient Divine Wisdom. No one can grasp It above, across, or in the middle. There is none equal to that One whose name is Great Glory."

"There is divine beauty in learning, just as there is human beauty in tolerance. To learn means to accept the postulate that life did not begin at my birth. Others have been here before me, and I walk in their footsteps. The books I have read were composed by generations of fathers and sons, mothers and daughters, teachers and disciples. I am the sum total of their experiences, their quests...and so are you."

"Oftentimes, one strips oneself of passion in order to see the Secret of Life. Oftentimes, one regards life with passion in order to see its manifest forms. These two, the Secret and its manifestations, are in their nature the same. They are given different names. When they become manifest They may both be called the Cosmic Mystery. Reaching from the Mystery into the Deeper Mystery is the Gate to the secret of All Life."

IS OUR SPIRITUAL PRACTICE BRINGING ABOUT TRANSFORMATION?

This dharma talk given by Anam Tulku Thubten on May 5th, 2006, was transcribed by Roslyn Stark in 2006, and edited by Babaji Bob Kindler for inclusion in Nectar of Nondual Truth by permission of the Dharmata Foundation.

There's no such place called hell where we are going to be reborn after we die. There are only two places: either paradise or limbo; but there's no hell. [laughter] So after all, nothing can really go wrong after we die.

But I think that limbo is already happening right now, before you die. It is that spiritual limbo wherein we are constantly being stuck with our own personal myths and fantasies. At the same time, there is a sense of hell as a mental state wherein we are very much bound into our own unfinished concepts, unfinished neuroses, unfinished *karmic* patterns. I think that is why Buddha often spoke about that, in other words, that the best of human life is filled with suffering. This is a very difficult concept to understand until we come to the realization that there are unpurified *karmic* abundances in our consciousness, and that they often appear to us as unnecessary suffering.

As a matter of fact, common to the recognition of that, suffering is perhaps the most important element in achieving a more genuine aspiration towards the *buddha-dharma*, the true spiritual path, and not just some kind of spiritual trip. There are sometimes in our lives that we are simply riding along on a spiritual pretense, and that does not bring about any true transformation at all. We have to realize that sooner or later. As long as we are not really working toward purifying our *karmic* patterns and having this very genuine and passionate love and aspiration towards the great awakening, then even though superficially, outwardly, we might be practicing spiritual disciplines, that may be just another spiritual trip that fails to bring about any transformation.

Of course what I'm saying is not always the most pleasant message, you see. And especially if you're under the impression "I'm on the right track and I'm evolving," you know, "because I have all these valid signs and reasons indicating that I'm evolving." And when we are under this false sentiment, then all this message that I'm delivering right now is always unpleasant. It's not pleasant to myself too sometimes, what I'm speaking about, but then the truth always forces you to speak the truth yourself, you see? Truth about ourselves, truth about our journey, our *dharma* practice.

The question that we have to often ask, then, is how many years we have been practicing *dharma* or even a formal discipline that could be a Buddhist practice, or that could be another form of meditation practice, and then how much have we really evolved? And how much the same problems we are still repeating and holding onto even today in this very moment? Ironically, we often discover that most of our problems are not new problems, right? They're old buddies, you see? Yes, they are very old friends who are extremely familiar with our consciousness. The same judgment that I'm experiencing today, for example, this very moment, costs me so much energy, costs me so much price, you see? I'm thinking of just one particular form of *klesha* here, like judgment. You realize that the same judgment has been tormenting you without any real purpose many times, countless times, and then today the very same judgment that is tormenting you for some reason is the same judgment that was experienced perhaps 20 years ago, 30 years ago; it's that same judgment!

In the same way, we can actually go through the whole inventory of the *kleshas*? Anger, jealousy, depression, self-hatred, the belief in duality, you see? All these *kleshas* are not new; they are actually very old. They are deep-seated habitual patterns which have been there all the way through life; perhaps all of them go back to past lifetimes, too. And regardless of the spiritual disciplines we have been practicing for the last 5 or 10 or 20 years, all these *kleshas* are being rejuvenated, they're getting stronger — it's as if as if they are on a very good diet. [laughter] They are going to the gym every day, you see? They are not weakening after all, and they're even stronger than ever in some sense. And now they're like viruses that end up developing all the strategies to counter the meditation methods that we have been applying. You know? So now the question is what should we do with them?

In the first place, as I said, we have to come to the acknowledgment that we are very much bound to all these habitual patterns in our consciousness, and that these have become a reservoir of unnecessary suffering. And suffering is not always conscious. It's very unconscious sometimes. It is like this hidden hell, lying in very deep dark realms or the hidden reaches of our consciousness which we don't have access to most of the time. And yet we experience it as an external symptom in daily life.

But then again, if you get at this matter from the perspective of the *buddha-dharma*, especially the *Vajrayana*, there is the possibility of not only lessening this internal conflict, but completely uprooting that conflict. And as I said last Sunday, after all this ceremony and *dharma* teachings, there's the possibility, even actual necessity, that we should be awakened eternally forever after that, because that's very possible.

And in a similar way, I believe that there are going to be some times of synchronicity, times of experiencing a genuine, pure luminous awareness, or awakening mind, when we meditate. We will gain that necessary prerequisite to bring about a great awakening on the spot — such as that passionate aspiration to be awakened. Also, the courage to acknowledge our own negativities, those habitual patterns of our minds. When we are able to have both of these, then it will become more than possible.

There must be a certainty that pure awareness happens when we meditate. When we sit on the meditation cushion, it occurs. And when that happens, we have to recognize that is that original, pure awareness, and not look to see anything else. We must know that it is the highest truth, that it is the most brilliant awareness that one can experience.

Anyway, I believe that when we come here together, by having that mindset, that pure mindset, that aspiration to be awakened and receptivity of the *dharma* teachings, the blessings of the *sangha*, then we always experience this pure luminous awareness. And sometimes this luminous awareness is very subtle; it does not come with a whole procession. There's no herald who blows a trumpet, no official that lights incense, no usher who tells you that this pristine awareness is coming into your house of consciousness. That seldom happens. Sometimes that awareness instantly blossoms, and just crops up in the middle of nowhere when you meditate, when you have that perfect mindset which I've been speaking about. And then awareness arises in things even most ordinary. And you have to know that is that luminous awareness, and reach it, and know that you are no longer being enslaved by those demonic forces of judgment, hatred, and dualism.

Then, the question is, how can we maintain that luminous awareness in our everyday life? And not just having a glimpse of it now and then. Otherwise, we are going to end up being *puja* addicts. Actually I'm discovering there is this element in me, being a *puja* addict, because when you come here you are also experiencing the luminous awareness. It is very contagious in a way that suddenly, brilliant light is turned on in the darkness of my consciousness. Then it's very easy to enter that dimension of perfect truth wherein everyone, everything, is already awakened, wherein there is no imperfection after all. But then that experience of awareness does not last long most of the time. That awareness does not have a very strong composure sometimes. Meeting with small challenges causes complete collapse of that awareness, that majestic composure, you see? It's like a coward can pretend to be heroic, but if he meets a very vicious cat he loses his composure. And we're like that, that coward hero who knows how to pretend all these composures, do all these heroic postures — jumping in the sky, and showing all this physical prowess, but the truth is if he meets a wild cat, he loses his composure, and runs.

And sometimes our awareness is like that. During the *puja* or in the prayers, in the *sangha* where everybody is experiencing this collective awareness, it's very easy for us to experience it, amazing brilliant awareness, which is genuine awareness in itself; there's nothing wrong with that. But the problem is if we leave the sanctuary, the *mandala*, and then sometimes we have to meet small challenges, like somebody cutting you off on the highway, then immediately the demon just rises up, we don't know from where, and cause that total collapse of awareness. It's a false composure in a way that your mindset can be drugged, can be enslaved by that inner demon, the demon of reaction, the demon of judgment, and then you're no longer that *bodhisattva* who was enjoying swimming in the heart and pool of that awareness. Rather, you become this monster having flames and fires coming out of your nostrils, you see? [laughter] And then you realize that you're transformed into the personality that you really despise as a spiritual person.

So today we really have to think about how can we maintain that awareness, in everyday life when we meet big challenges as well as small challenges. And this seems more important; in fact this determines whether we are a real *dharma* practitioner or not. This title, *dharma* practitioner, it's very nice, a safe title without too much side effects, without too many special trappings. Because there are other titles that carry lots of negative side effects. Like titles such as *lama* or *dakini* or *khandro*. There are some titles that have lots of negative effect. But the *dharma* practitioner is one of those few titles that don't have any negative effects. So I really identify myself as *dharma* practitioner. It has very particular meaning, and that conveys our ultimate formidable assignment, which means we're not just somebody who has a little bit of curiosity about spirituality or who goes to temple now and then, like Sunday church-goers. But rather, we are somebody who is practicing the art of luminous awareness, and realizing it in each and every moment.

Buddhist teachings say that once you become a *dharma* practitioner, you have to maintain this responsibility, not only during meditation, not only while you're awake, but even while you're sleeping. Even when you are having a dream. In those states you have to maintain that work, the work of maintaining awareness constantly. Because if you lose awareness one second, that's where that inner demon of negative forces can cause this complete relapse again, and take you into ordinary place where you feel that you have never been practicing meditation, you have never practiced *dharma* before.

Let me share some of my personal experiences. Sometimes there are moments where you lose awareness just for a single moment while you're having this moment-to-moment awareness, and feeling that you're already awakened, and feeling that you have something to share with other people. You really feel that you have this tremendous gift that you can share with other people. Now and then you feel that sense of, 'Oh I'm having this luminous awareness, and at least once last month I didn't have any major problems; I didn't have any noticeable judgment or hatred in my consciousness. Now I feel I'm especially gifted, and I can share with other people. [laughter] And it's a very good feeling because now you're coming to this conclusion that you're not only not evil, but you may also have this gift of Christ, or Buddha, that you can help other people. But then you can lose awareness one moment

> "There must be a certainty that pure awareness happens when we meditate. When we sit on the meditation cushion, it occurs. And when that happens, we have to recognize that is that original, pure awareness, and not look to see anything else. We must know that it is the highest truth, that it is the most brilliant awareness that one can experience."

and that gift disappears, and the absence of awareness plus the presence of this ego, this ultimate demon, returns and drives you all the way back to where you started. Then you feel that you can easily be beaten by the demons of the *kleshas*. You feel that you're ordinary or confused, and that basically you haven't achieved any awakening; you haven't achieved any true realization.

This is ok. As *dharma* students, we have to expect that there are going to be many ups and downs in our journey where we are going to lose completely our luminous awareness and full possession of the moment awareness.

But this should not be another devious reason that we should lose faith in ourselves or give up our hope, our aspiration. As a matter of fact, these now-and-then-ups and downs of our journey should be one of the many reasons to convince ourself that we really should dedicate our life and our energy towards the cultivation of *buddha-dharma*, because this is the obvious reason that we still have *kleshas*, habitual patterns, that haven't been purified in our consciousness. And as long as we are keeping them alive, then there's no way we can experience complete transformation. We're going to be subject to misery and suffering either in this lifetime or the next lifetime. And so that kind of relapse of realization should convince us to dedicate our life to the work of the holy *dharma*, which is the work of awareness as the number one work, as the highest vocation in our life.

Also it is truly necessary to dedicate a certain amount of time every day to a formal meditation practice, because when you practice formal meditation, including sitting meditation or *sadhana*, it immediately brings you back to the awareness. If at least you can experience some sense of a pure luminous awareness, definitely you will experience aspiration. And you're going to have this awareness, some kind of awareness that you can see why you should be practicing *buddha-dharma*. And you're able to also have a sense of light or recognition, and a mindfulness regarding the very negative force holding you back from evolving.

Therefore, practicing a formal meditation every day is imperative, very necessary. Without having some kind of ongoing daily assignment like *dharma* practice, I feel that there is no other way that one can really successfully break down these habitual patterns. It is true that when you come to *pujas* or when you sit sometimes in the presence of the *sangha*, or in the presence of other meditators, you can sometimes experience amazing luminous awareness, but that doesn't last long.

So I really hope you understand that this is not about having that kind of now-and-then immediate, wonderful, mindblowing spiritual experience. You can have an abnormal mindblowing experience by traveling into exotic places, or jumping out of an airplane with parachute, but how many times you can jump out of an airplane with a parachute? Maybe a few times in your lifetime. You know you can't do that every day, each and every moment. So if you are completely satisfied, if you decide that's enough for you — having that kind of momentary luminous awareness, then it's like jumping off an airplane with a parachute; You are looking for a way of blowing your mind, and that's all. You are merely impressing yourself.

And there are people who do that, you know. People say, "Oh, did you see that such and such a master is visiting town tomorrow? We should go there, yeah?" And you can get a bunch of people who come with you as if you are going to a movie, or going to a restaurant, and then you all can have that positively amazing spiritually and nourishing experience by being in the presence of a *guru* or spiritual master. And then that master leaves you for another town and may never come back, or if he comes back, maybe it takes one year. And you go there and you can become completely infatuated again by that experience. And finally you decide to hang a pin-up of that *guru* on your altar, you see? And all the while you remain as the helpless prisoner of all your conflicts and problems, right? You keep judging yourself, judging other people, and having all this conflict that is simply the production of your unawakened consciousness, you see?

So I'm not really saying that we should not put pictures of *gurus* on our altar, that we should not now and then have a wonderful spiritual experience by joining a *guru* or attending teachings or initiations. What I'm saying is that there is a fundamental necessity in our journey which is to keep maintaining *dharma* practice every day of our life.

And more than that, it is truly necessary to maintain a formal meditation practice, doing either sitting meditation or *sadhana* practice, once every day. If not twice every day, then once every day of your life. Because otherwise we can fool ourselves by thinking we don't have to practice once every day or twice every day, because now we realize the truth. Or I have a glimpse of awakening. Or I'm a *dzogchen* master, or I'm a *dzogchen* practitioner. So I really don't have to do all this foundational practice, I don't have to do this kind of work. This is not for me. This is for people who are not so awakened, or they are for *dharma* dummies. You see? [laughter]

This can be a very subtle way of manipulating ourselves. So if we really don't want to falsely manipulate ourselves, then we have to practice *dharma* every day of our life. And doing the *sadhana* or the sitting meditation once every day. It's like showering your consciousness. I've been giving this as an analogy to encourage all of us to practice meditation or the *sadhana* every day. Practicing the

> " ....these now and then ups and downs of our journey should be one of the many reasons to convince ourself that we really should dedicate our life and our energy towards the cultivation of *buddha-dharma*, because this is the obvious reason that we still have *kleshas*, habitual patterns, that haven't been purified in our consciousness."

dharma, the work of meditation is like taking a shower. It's like a spiritual shower. Once every day, a spiritual shower. It's truly necessary. Otherwise there will be lots of bacteria, like termites – neurotic termites that literally eat our consciousness. When we are completely gripped by the force of our *kleshas*, it's like termites eating our consciousness, you see? Our consciousness gets stale, gets rotten, and then we begin to inflict unnecessary pain upon our consciousness as well as the consciousness of other people too.

Practicing the *dharma* every day of your life is not really arduous at all! This has nothing to do with sacrificing or compromising your life or your daily responsibilities. It's not really about that you give up your work or you become celibate or you dedicate a huge portion of your time in everyday life to the work of *dharma*. Or it has nothing to do with all kinds of really difficult, elaborate austerities which involve self-torment. Not at all! I'm not asking everybody to do some kind of very difficult meditation practice where you have to stand ten times a day on your head in your living room; that is both difficult and futile, right? Or stand still for five hours every day, or to do a silly meditation that involves a hodgepodge of inferior methods. The work that I'm speaking about is really simple. Sometimes it's so simple that all you need to do is just sit and be quiet; that's all you need to do.

Did you see this blue book we have been contributing to everybody in the *sangha*, as well as to other people who take refuge vows; it's very simple text. I have been contributing the book to everybody who took refuge vows, and now we're out of inventory, right? It's very small book. It has only like three pages or four pages. It can be reduced into one page if you like, actually. It looks nicer from an artistic viewpoint, so we made that into books because it's much nicer to give a book than give just one sheet, one piece of paper. And also, people tend to take it more respectfully when it's in the form of a book instead of just the one piece of paper. Those few prayers I have divided into different pages and we made this beautiful very handy blue-colored book. I have been giving that to everybody. And sometimes people say, really is this enough? Please give me more *sadhana*, or something that has more page numbers. And of course when you're ready, you can do the *sadhana* with many page numbers if you like. But what I'm trying to say is that practice really does not require a large quantity, or lots of effort. Practice does not have to be arduous or self-tormenting or complicated at all!

So, I think that one of the mistakes we make in our relationship to *dharma* practice is that either we don't do, or, if we do, we need something very complicated. You see? That seems to be one of the very familiar problems we face in *dharma* practice. Somehow there's a way that we can completely ignore this notion that *dharma* practice can be simple and be affordable, while it is also work that you can practice every day, cultivate every day, like you have to eat food every day. You have to breathe each and every moment. Awareness is like air, literally. If you don't breathe your air, then you're going to suffer, you're going to feel uncomfortable. It is the same if you don't breathe the air of awareness; you're going to be suffering, you're going to be suffocating eventually. And that's how important and nourishing awareness is to our consciousness. Awareness comes into being when you engage in the work of *buddha-dharma*.

So finally the *buddha-dharma* can be very simple, as long as you realize that the importance of the *dharma* practice is the same as importance of taking shower every day or breathing each and every moment. Then it's really simple. Because it has nothing to do with quantity. It has to do with the fact that you have this complete realization of the importance of the *buddha-dharma*, and realizing that this is the highest work. Because there's no work in this life that can bring about the inner happiness, the inner transformation, besides the *dharma* practice.

You know, we tried everything, right? We tried all kinds of methods to satisfy our egos and to be happy and to be fulfilled. We tried almost everything that is available to us. However, it was the ego; we tried to gain fulfillment and a sense of satisfaction by doing everything that our ego told us to do, and all the while believing in all of this social myth.

Social myth, after all, is a great deception to all of us. When I say social myth, I'm speaking about the value system that exists in this society. It's not like simply reading a book, or reading newspapers, or some kind of text containing these social values. The social myth is actually a belief system that gets entrenched in our mind very deep over time. So now there's this mental print of all these unenlightened belief systems in our consciousness, all basically telling us that happiness and fulfillment do not lie within us, they lie outside of us. They also tell us that this moment is not adequate, that this moment is always inadequate. Who you are is always inadequate. The essence of this moment as well as the essence of who you are at this very moment is inadequate. The only way that you can be adequate or that you can find the purpose of your life is by acquiring success, or money, or pleasure.

So we have tried all of them basically, all of these possible means to satisfy our ego. And now we realize there is nothing in this world that can bring about ultimate happiness. And after we have been defeated and failed so many times by not getting what we really want to get, even though we have been doing it all exactly in accordance with the laws dictated by these conventional values, then we have failed, right?

And then we realize that we have to be spiritual. I have got to do Buddhist practice. How about I read the Common Ground newspaper, right? Common Ground? Is there anything in that magazine that can solve your problems? So, you come to know that you have to follow some kind of spiritual principle, because nothing is working. And in this mindset you might lose your relationship, or contract a serious illness, or you have some kind of emotional breakdown. In the face of all this you kind of pick up something helpful in the spiritual path and may get temporary benefit from it. But in the interim we forgot again that we have been defeated recently, that we have failed again in the process of actualizing ultimate happiness or fulfillment due to doing everything with an unawakened mind And all these irrational and mistaken belief systems go on dictating to us what we are supposed to do in the back of our minds. How can we actualize happiness until we rid ourselves of that memory of defeat?

So it's very good to remember now and then that we have been defeated many times. It does not mean that we are going to

> "There's nothing wrong with having a nice life at all. A nice life is never a sin, actually. As a matter of fact, we have two responsibilities: we have a mundane responsibility and we have a dharmic responsibility, and they both are necessary. Sometimes one cannot really exist without the other."

renounce everything by tomorrow morning, like after you hear this lecture you go back and start packing your suitcase and retire into the mountains. Not at all! Of course we are going to maintain our life style as before. We are going to do everything to the very best of our abilities, trying to succeed There's nothing wrong with having a nice life at all. A nice life is never a sin, actually. As a matter of fact, we have two responsibilities: we have a mundane responsibility and we have a *dharmic* responsibility, and they both are necessary. Sometimes one cannot exist without the other. You see? But that's where we forgot that our *dharmic* responsibility, the responsibility of discovering and awakening is our ultimate vocation. We completely forgot that when we end up worshiping blindly those value systems dictated by an unawakened society, we stand little chance of fully awakening our consciousness. And then we're almost doomed to suffer. And so, it is very good to remember that we have been defeated many times.

Actually, we don't have to make any major changes. The only change we have to make is simply start practicing *dharma* as the work of meditation, the work of awareness. Practicing *dharma* is not like going to the hospital, or going to a conventional therapist who is a part of that social myth in order to fix your problems. That costs tremendous money, right? You think that maybe you will find that latest technology which solves all problems. But you can't afford that technology. If you can afford that technology, maybe you will have to read this very complicated manual that requires a Ph.D. in science, or something like that. As a matter of fact, our consciousness is completely permeated by problems. But to transcend those problems does not require any further complications. It only requires *dharma* practice, which is very simple.

Dharma practice can be reduced to this very simple method of pausing; giving yourself time to pause, then just keep pausing. That's all I can say: *dharma* is actually the art of pausing, after all. When you pause, awareness arises, because awareness is already there. As Longchenpa talks about it, *"Don't do anything,"* he said. Don't do anything. If you leave your consciousness as it is then all the elements diluting your consciousness will go away, will vanish automatically. It is like, when you leave water alone when it is polluted, eventually all the things that are polluting it go away, all that sediment will start sinking down and the water will become clear.

And in the same way if you just pause and leave your consciousness as it is, without fantasizing the future or replaying the past or chasing after thought or trying to strike conversation with your neuroses, if you just leave it completely, totally, without doing anything, without doing anything, both voluntarily and involuntarily, then all will become clear.

If you know how to pause completely, then awareness arises. It's amazing, and in that clarity you can perceive your own habitual patterns in a detached way. You also realize this very merciless bloody truth that perhaps you have been deceived; you have been enslaved by your own mind, your own unawakened consciousness for all that time. You realize that too. You realize that actually your own unawakened mind is responsible for causing all these headaches, all this unnecessary sorrow. You now see, as well, that there was no one in your life who caused you pain, who caused you suffering; in other words, you cannot point your finger to any other person or condition, no matter how unsuccessful, unfavorable they were or are. They now appear as your own ordinary perspective. You cannot point your finger to them as objects of blame.

At first its a very awful awakening, because now you feel that you've done something wrong to yourself. "Oh, really? I'm the one who has been torturing myself?" You see? That cannot be true! Right? "I don't think I am an idiot like that. I don't think I'm so deluded as that." You see? That's why I call it a bloody awful truth to be discovered. "Is it really true that I can't blame anybody anymore? That's terrible if it is! If it's true that I'm not supposed to react to any conditions from this moment on? I'm supposed to maintain this sobering awareness, being still, calm, and never reacting to any changes? And simply telling myself that all problems are illusory, simply productions of my mind? From this moment until I die?"

This is something we didn't really think about carefully, right, after all? [laughter] After all these years of studying *dharma*, you see, you really didn't uncover this message that I'm speaking about; seriously we didn't think about, right? It's like buying nice house. It's beautiful. It has a nice garage, big garage; you can put three cars together if you want. And there is this very nice neighbor. Everybody around you is wealthy, you know, all the neighbors; and there's no crime. It has a beautiful lawn. It's like the ultimate American dream. No wonder that you have this strong impulse that you want to buy it. And if somehow you are able to buy it, you really didn't think so much about maintaining the lawn and paying mortgages, and trouble with the neighbors, did you? You don't think carefully about all these things when you buy it.

Practicing *dharma* is like that sometimes. When you get into dharma practice, this *dharma* becomes very attractive, and very seductive, actually. It is truly beautiful. The whole idea of becoming enlightened, liberating all sentient beings, you see? And perhaps your first impression of *dharma* must be something very impressive for you. It is very impressive to your understanding of what is happening right now.

So nothing terrible is happening right now. We are all sitting here. It looks like we are all the chosen people, in some sense. [laughter] And so far we have had all these powerful meditation practices, reciting sacred sounds, and really thinking about all these issues that ordinary people even don't know how to think about. So this can be very impressive for your mind.

> "From this moment on we should never react to any condition. It's absolutely illegal, you see? [laughter] We're not supposed to react to any unfavorable condition — even if you run into very unwanted circumstances, even if you get into a car accident in a few days, and then you realize that your insurance expired just a few days before that, you are not allowed to react. We're not supposed to react in any way that may turn our precious consciousness hellish and miserable."

So therefore I believe the *dharma* can be very impressive and seductive in the beginning, as you come close to *dharma* for the first time in your life. It's very easy to get into this whole journey in the same way that it's very easy to have this impulse of buying that nice house. And when you really start practicing *dharma* truthfully, then there is this awesome responsibility. From this moment on we should never react to any condition. It's illegal, absolutely, you see? [laughter] We're not supposed to react to any unfavorable condition — even if you run into very unwanted circumstances, even if you get into a car accident in a few days, and then you realize that your insurance expired just a few days before that, you are not allowed to react. We're not supposed to react in any way that may turn our precious consciousness hellish and miserable. Otherwise we may start beating ourselves up day and night and telling ourselves that this is awful in a way that you can completely distort reality.

Actually, one teacher said that reality is like beautiful glass. You can paint anything you like to paint on it. You can paint a monster on it too. Or you can leave the glass alone. It is beautiful glass which is always perfect in each and every moment. You also have the choice to paint that glass a black color, white color, red color, green color. You can paint a beautiful image, like an image of flowers. Or an image of Buddha. It's your choice. And now you have to come to this realization that you have a choice always to paint that glass, which is reality. Your mind has this power, this capability of either distorting or painting reality the way you want, the way you wish.

Actually, one of the powerful convictions I had made me believe that the Buddha's teaching is infallible, because Buddha's teaching is very hard to accept, after all. Let me tell you why it's so difficult to accept Buddha's teachings. Buddha's teachings offer the ultimate challenge to us as the spiritual work to be done. Buddha's teaching teaches that everything is the creation of our own mind. That's a very difficult truth to accept, you see. Because it doesn't seem that everything is the production of my mind, after all. Of course, when we are happy, when we are having a good experience of being in la-la-land, it's very easy to believe this truth. Oh yeah, everything is the production of my mind, you see. Because we can strike the bottom in our life, when something goes wrong with our life, and especially if there is this misfortune in life in terms of having serious tragedies, one after another, to the extent of even having a major crisis of life. Maybe you realize that your child is doing drugs. Or you realize that perhaps, your partner is cheating on you. Or you realize that you have a terminal cancer. Then, at that time, it's really difficult to accept that everything is manifested of your own mind. It's very hard to say that, you see. I think it's one reason I'm telling everybody that it's so hard to really believe in Buddha's teaching. It's very easy to believe teachings other than Buddha's teachings. It's easy to believe all this mythology about a God, about an evil devil, devils, and such; it's very easy to believe in them — much easier to believe in them. So it's difficult to really believe what Buddha taught when it comes down to the place that we meet these ultimate challenges.

But when we read Buddha's teachings on paper, it's very easy for us to think, "Oh: this is exactly what I've been thinking about. I have heard this expression from many people when they came to Buddhist teachings or one day they picked up a Buddhist text for the first time in their life. That's what I was thinking about when I was a child, when I was 8 years old, when I was 10 years old. I had the exact understanding of life and the death that the Buddha taught." Or, as a movie star might say, "Maybe I was the reincarnation of some Tibetan lama in a past life." Because the Buddha's teachings are very trendy in some ways, but very scientific in other ways.

So, you see, that's why a growing number of people are surfacing every month who are very much liking Buddha's teachings, because Buddha's teachings are very cool. As a matter of fact, I read an article recently that many scientists are becoming very fascinated by Buddha's teachings, because they realize that Buddhism is one of the few religions that can go along with modern science. Not traditional science, but more cutting-edge science without any conflict. So that's why when you read the Buddha's teachings, it makes sense. That's why you see so many psychologists desperate to try to steal some ideas from Buddhism. [laughter] They're trying to make their work look better, and more suitable, or more workable, more financially succesful, because they realize that their work is not really helping people in a powerful way.

But the truth is that, it's easy to believe Buddha's teachings when you have a full belly and beautiful weather, when everything's kind of going well, no major tragedies, with little problems that are ok. Then it's very easy to think, "Ahh, I really believe what Buddha taught as a matter of fact; I really believe that what Buddha taught is the truth. Is the truth: everything is a manifestation of my mind, obviously. But then something else comes, and you are forced to meet the greatest challenges. Then there is the question, "Can I sit there gracefully and not lose my love, not lose my humanity and my compassion for all beings? And not lose my patience, and my forgiveness, and my kindness towards everyone around me, including myself? And simply be able to deal with all problems gracefully. And at same time, not lose this conviction, this realization that everything is my mind. Can I do that? Everything is my mind?"

Imagine that you're locked up in some really serious, horrifying situation. Let's say, if I imagine I was in Second World War, if

> "Once you identify with awareness, then there's no space in your consciousness where you can grow, and thus no place where you can harbor those old habitual patterns anymore. They're completely gone forever. They reach their ultimate and eternal demise."

I imagine I was a Jewish person and I was locked up in a concentration camp, would I be able to simply remember this wisdom, this simple truth, that everything is my mind. Can I simply keep my awakening mind in that ultimate and unconditional love towards all these Nazis who are trying to kill me, who are despising my race; can I do that? Or would I say, true, right now I don't believe what Buddha taught, but when everything gets better, then I'm going to believe what Buddha taught. That's what we're doing sometimes, you know. We're like good-weather Buddhists sometimes. When the weather is good I'm going to believe what Buddha taught, but when the weather is not good, I'm going to allow my mind to change.

But let me give you another example. Imagine that you are facing a very serious issue. Whatever that can be. It can be a very horrifying car accident. The car accident that has occurred to you and that has caused injury to your body is not really a state of your mind. It's real. That is what is happening out there. And we cannot deny that. If you deny that, that's simply denying truth again. But then there is thought which has nothing to do with awareness, thought that is usually very judgmental and very unawakened. That thought lies in your unawakened perception that you immediately developed when trying to explain and trying to interpret what has happened right now, just a few seconds ago, and which is always a form of either thought or concept. Those thoughts are sending you this message, this very negative, destructive message in your consciousness, telling you that all that has happened is terrible; it's awful, it's ruined your life. Now you don't have much hope, and you should be suffering. You should be angry towards yourself, and you should be angry at whatever has occurred. You should be so angry that you should also be more destructive now that you don't have any hope, or you don't have any goodness in your life. That thought has actually nothing to do with what happened. That thought has nothing to do with what has occurred. That thought is this manifestation of your unawakened consciousness that is habitual; that is simply *karmic*.

And now we can apply the same analogy in relationship to everything that is going on around you right now. Today, this moment, before I end this teaching, I want everybody to pick out a condition that you are resisting right now. I'm sure there is something you don't like, something that is happening right now. I want everybody to visualize it for a while, in your mind. It can be anything. It can be the fact I'm getting old, or the fact that I'm having a huge financial crisis, or the fact that I don't like the way I look, or the fact that I have lots of guilt associated with the past. Or I have lots of fear associated with the future, with death, with illness. It is time to bring about awareness and direct it towards all this resistance and fear which is destroying your attempts to settle into that peaceful, compassionate awareness.

Now two things are happening. Actually nothing is happening right now in this moment. Everything's perfect, right? And that's perhaps the truth, after all. But even if something is happening, there are two things happening: what is happening, and how you are responding to it. However, in this moment everything's perfect. Look into this situation and analyse it like this.

If you keep maintaining that awareness which I'm speaking about, by "pausing," then you'll find that there is this inexpressible awareness. It can be called truth. It can be called your buddha-nature. And if you can be with that, if you can recognize that as your true essence, then, in that luminous awareness which is your true identity you will no longer be subject to any causes, conditions, or circumstances in your life. You can have a financial crisis, you can have a terminal illness, none of those circumstances can injure or can cause harm to your luminous awareness.

The first thing when you practice meditation is, you must realize that there is this amazing luminous awareness existing in your consciousness, and that you haven't discovered it before. It is as if you were sitting on a whole bag of gold all the while yet you have been feeling poor for the last 50 years, and suddenly you came to this realization with a tremendous sense of surprise – "Oh, actually I wasn't poor; I've been wealthy. I just didn't look in the right place!" But then once you discover that, this luminous awareness, and through stabilizing that in your consciousness, eventually all your false identities, all your false belief systems will begin to fall apart, and to the extent that you begin to identify yourself as that awareness – then you have begun to realize that you are awareness.

Once you realize that you are awareness, then there's no longer any need of your cultivating meditation practice. There's no longer any need of trying to produce or trying to acquire that awareness, because now you have become awareness. When you become awareness, then finally you become awakened. Once you identify with awareness, then there's no space in your consciousness where you can grow, and thus no place where you can harbor those old habitual patterns anymore. They're completely gone forever. They reach their ultimate and eternal demise.

Thank you, everybody.

ANAM THUBTEN grew up in Tibet and at an early age began to practice in the Nyingma tradition of Tibetan Buddhism. He is the founder and spiritual advisor of the Dharmata Foundation, and he teaches widely in the United States and internationally.

Tathagatagarbha / Atman – Transparency of the Self

akase'va sakuntanam gati tesham durannaya
"The actions of an Arhat are without trace, trackless — like birds flying through the sky."
Lord Buddha

Subtle Indications of a Tathagagata
- No foundation for an individual self
- Free of conditioned phenomena
- Transcendent of men, gods, and mara
- Free of suffering and other burdens
- Free of mental projections and emotions
- Abandonment of the 5 Skandhas

Manjushri Nama-Sangit:
- The Pervasive Self
- The Supreme Self
- Buddha Self
- Self that is the Source of All
- The Beginningless Self
- The Diamond Self
- The Self of Substance
- Guardian Self of the Three Worlds
- The Single Self
- The Holy Immovable Self
- Self of Primordial Purity
- Self of Thus-ness

"The root of all beings is nothing else but one Self. I am that place in which all existence resides."
Samantrabadra, All-Creating King Tantra

"Each sentient being contains the intrinsic indwelling potency for becoming a Buddha – fully awakened." Lord Buddha

The meaning of the word, Tathagatagarbha:
tatha – thus; gata – the Goal beyond coming and going; garbha – root, essence

"Tathagatagarbha is not 'I' or 'me,' is stationary and immovable though appearing and vanishing, transcends the human condition, is what really is – suchness – and is the ultimate Goal."

"The Universal Self sports through entities via Samadhi. It performs deeds and works while stationed at one immovable post."
Guhya Samaja Tantra

PROF. LARRY A. HERZBERG

RELIGIOUS BELIEFS AS FOUNDATIONAL
ONE WAY OF RESPONDING TO A QUESTIONING FRIEND

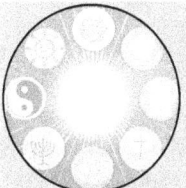

Have you ever been asked by a friend, "Why do you believe that?," where 'that' refers to a core religious belief, such as that God exists? Assuming that your friend is genuinely curious and not just trying to goad you, there are several ways you might choose to respond. One would be to cite a good practical consequence of your religious belief, or of your practicing your religion more broadly, such as that it comforts you, or makes you more compassionate. Another, which would be more appropriate if your friend happened to be scientifically-minded, would be to provide evidence of your belief's truth. After all, your scientifically-minded friend is really asking you to justify your religious belief by providing non-religious beliefs that support it or express reasons for thinking it is true. For many such "evidentialists," your justification would have to include some beliefs about the world that could be verified or confirmed by ordinary sense perceptions. By contrast, a more philosophically-minded friend might be asking for a purely logical proof to support your religious belief. Certain well-known Western philosophers like Anselm, Aquinas, and Descartes have attempted such proofs, and recently some philosophers have tried to update them in order to make them more convincing to non-religious but still open-minded seekers of knowledge.

Both the traditional and updated proofs that God exists rely upon what their authors consider to be axioms (such as "Whatever begins to exist has a cause"), which are intended to play a privileged or foundational role in the process of gaining knowledge of any type. After all, such philosophers argue, if every belief required evidential support, we would never attain any knowledge because we would be endlessly called upon to provide evidence to support any previously offered evidence. But this raises an important question in the context of proofs of religious beliefs: if, as "foundationalists" hold, all knowledge necessarily requires an axiomatic foundation, then, instead of trying to prove religious beliefs on a foundation of non-religious axioms, why not simply consider religious beliefs themselves to be foundational axioms? If you were to take this sort of approach, your friend's question about why you believe that God exists could be dispensed with quickly. You could just reply, "No reason. I have no evidence for it, but that's because it doesn't require any; I find it to be foundational." But of course, this may not satisfy your curious friend, because they may now worry about how to draw the line between foundational axioms and non-foundational beliefs. Without some reasonable limits, couldn't a jurist at a trial just ignore all evidence to the contrary and merely assert that their belief in the defendant's guilt or innocence is foundational for them? One way of responding to this sort of concern has been offered by the influential Christian philosopher Alvin Plantinga, who taught philosophy at the University of Notre Dame for more than thirty years. If you are interested in exploring his ideas more deeply, you could begin by reading his books *Rationality and Religious Belief* and *Faith and Rationality*. Here I will just try to briefly summarize his views as they relate to the question at hand.

Plantinga begins from the idea that the beliefs in each of our minds are organized into a "noetic structure" in which they are related to each other in various ways. For instance, many beliefs in this structure draw evidential or explanatory support from other beliefs, but others are foundational or "basic" in the sense that they are not formed or supported by other beliefs. Each belief in one's noetic structure is also ordered by how firmly one holds the belief, or by the degree of confidence one places in it. Finally, some beliefs are more important to the structure than others, in that some (metaphorically, those on the edge) could easily be rejected without many others being affected, while those at the center would, if rejected, force one to abandon a multitude of other beliefs. For instance, I could easily give up my belief that I ate granola for breakfast yesterday without that affecting many other beliefs (although I might have to adjust the degree of confidence I place in other beliefs based on my memories), but I could not reject my belief that 1+1=2 without abandoning literally an infinite number of other beliefs.

Foundationalists disagree with non-foundationalists (commonly called "coherentists") over the sorts of noetic structures a rational person should have. They hold that the noetic structure of a rational person must be built upon a foundation of "basic" beliefs that do not require evidence, while coherentists deny this, holding that there is no such thing as a basic belief; all beliefs are evidentially supported by other beliefs, which in turn provide such support for other beliefs. Although the disagreement between these two schools of thought is a major fault line in the philosophy of knowledge (as it is practiced in the West), Plantinga recognizes that there is plenty of room for debate within each of them. Foundationalists disagree among themselves mainly over the question of which sorts of belief are basic. He notes that those he calls "ancient/medieval foundationalists" insist that a belief is basic for a person only if either it is self-evident to them or else it is immediately evident to their senses. Self-evident beliefs may be identified partly by the way they seem in the mind of the believer. For instance, John Locke, the famous British philosopher, suggested that they have "an evident luster", while Descartes described them as being "clear and distinct". On the other hand, beliefs that are evident to the senses are somewhat less mysterious; they are simply common beliefs about the perceivable world, like "There is a tree." Modern foundationalists tend to be more cautious in this regard. They hold that a belief is basic only if it is about the ways things seem to the believer (such as "I seem to see a tree"). They call these beliefs about the ways things seem "incorrigible", by which they mean that it would be pointless for anyone to disagree with the believer about their truth. Plantinga calls both modern and ancient/medieval foundationalists "classical", and he argues that

> "....if, as 'foundationalists' hold, all knowledge necessarily requires an axiomatic foundation, then, instead of trying to prove religious beliefs on a foundation of non-religious axioms, why not simply consider religious beliefs themselves to be foundational axioms? If you were to take this sort of approach, your friend's question about why you believe that God exists could be dispensed with quickly. You could just reply, 'No reason. I have no evidence for it, but that's because it doesn't require any; I find it to be foundational.'"

such classical foundationalism is too narrow and must be expanded if foundationalism is to be a viable view at all.

Plantinga begins to explain what he finds to be wrong with classical foundationalism by noting first that it seems to arbitrarily exclude from the foundations of knowledge certain sorts of very common but highly significant non-religious beliefs, such as the belief that there are conscious people in the world other than me. He insists that although this belief is "basic" for him (that is, he does not infer it from other beliefs), it does not meet any of the criteria of basicality set by classical foundationalism: he finds it to be neither self-evident, nor evident to his senses, nor incorrigible (because, true or false, it is not about a way things seem to him, but is rather about a way they are). He then makes his most important point against classical foundationalism, namely that it is "self-referentially inconsistent", by which he means that, as a belief, classical foundationalism is neither basic nor non-basic by its own criteria. It is not non-basic because it is not supported by other beliefs, and it is not basic (according to its own criteria of basicality) because it is not self-evident, evident to the senses, or incorrigible. So, by its own criteria of basicality, it would be irrational for a classical foundationalist to be a classical foundationalist.

This does not mean that Plantinga thinks that foundationalism should be abandoned in favor of coherentism. Rather, he draws inspiration from Calvinist and other Reformed objectors to the "natural theology" of Anselm, Aquinas, Descartes and others who tried without success (in his view) to prove the existence of God from other beliefs, some of which they considered to be basic. The Reformed objectors observed that their holy scriptures did not contain any such proofs; rather, they proceeded from God's existence as their starting point. Plantinga also notes that Calvin held that the belief that God exists is both innate and universal, and that this is doubted only due to the existence of sin (or, if one rejects the concept of sin, I suppose that one could blame sheer ignorance). In fact, Calvin held that a Christian ought not to believe in the existence of God on the basis of rational argument, since doing so would likely result in an unstable belief. After all, a belief established by one argument can in principle be overthrown by another.

While Plantinga does not argue that we should all be Calvinists, he takes the "central insight" of such Reformed thought to be that belief in God's existence is itself "properly basic". That is, as with the beliefs held by classical foundationalists to be basic, Plantinga argues that it is quite rational to believe that God exists without relying on support from any other beliefs (or even experiences, if Calvin is right about the belief's innateness).

However, this leaves open the worry about there being no limits on which beliefs one may properly find basic. Plantinga calls this "the Great Pumpkin Objection": if a belief in God can be considered properly basic, then why not a belief in the Great Pumpkin (a creature that Linus, a character in Charles Schultz's Peanuts cartoons, firmly believes to appear every Halloween)? Plantinga responds to this worry not by coming up with a more inclusive set of general criteria that could be used to tell basic from non-basic beliefs (which might be as self-referentially inconsistent as those of classical foundationalism), but rather by suggesting that we compare candidates for "proper basicality" to core examples by their similarities and dissimilarities. The core examples could include those that satisfy the criteria of classical foundationalism, but should also include other examples that are very widely held, such as the belief that there are conscious people in the world other than oneself. Plantinga admits that following this procedure would probably result in diverse criteria of basicality in different communities of believers, but he considers that to be all well and good. For most monotheistic communities, the belief that God exists would surely satisfy the criteria so developed. He concludes by noting, "Of course [someone who accepts this approach] is committed to supposing that there is a relevant difference between belief in God and belief in the Great Pumpkin... But this should prove no great embarrassment; there are plenty of candidates."

This foundationalist approach to answering the question "Why do you believe that?" may or may not satisfy your curious friend, of course. But it might allow you to avoid entering into an endless and possibly contentious debate about the truth of whatever non-religious beliefs or experiences one supposedly must have to support one's religious belief.

Larry A. Herzberg is a Professor of Philosophy at the University of Wisconsin – Oshkosh, where he teaches The Philosophy of Religion and Theory of Knowledge (Epistemology), among many other courses.

"GODBLOGS," CONTINUED
"Brahman-Bytes" in the Aftermath of the Avatar's Descent

This fresh installment of "Godblogs" helps to fill out the content of Nectar's thirty-eighth issue with profound seed sayings and stories from Sri Ramakrishna, the Avatar of the Age. Sparse though the words of a luminary are or may be, they never fail to transmit the power with which to disperse darkness and thin out the mind's ignorance — all in a simple manner. The knower of Divine Wisdom will never underestimate this force held within words — written or spoken — particularly when they are uttered by an illumined soul with a mind to free all beings from the illusion of bondage."

The Pulse of Spiritual Life
The Guru's Assessment of Spiritual Health....or Illness

Speaking on behalf of the art of teaching, and especially for the support and encouragement of all gurus who take up the onerous task of helping people neutralize their *karmas*, Sri Ramakrishna has spun many a story based on analogies of everyday life. Utilizing the principle of healing, and the doctors who

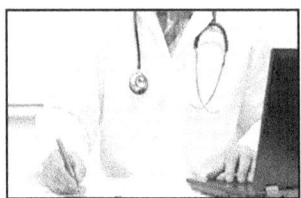

practice that art, he often talked about the superior, mediocre, and inferior doctors, i.e., *gurus*, the seeker may come upon in daily life. Relatedly, he said, "*One can understand the pulse of bile and phlegm only by living with a doctor.*"

To a doctor who holds one's arm and detects a subtle pulse by touching the wrist with a few fingers, or listens to the beating of the heart through a stethoscope, or glances down the throat after applying a tongue depressor, much gets revealed about the state of health of the patient. Importantly, one has to be present in the doctor's office and submit oneself to examination to reap the benefits of his experience — what to speak of gaining a valuable prognosis and receiving proper treatment. In similar fashion, the aspirant after Enlightenment, seeking nothing less than that all-important "Truth of Life and Existence," must subject the self (ego/mind mechanism) to constant examination in the light of the higher Awareness that verily emanates from the *guru's* very personage.

In this age-old process, called the *guru/shishya* relationship, first an overall examination of the aspirant's ongoing life and *karmas* from past lifetimes must occur. After that, along with any corrective measures the teacher sees and advises, the subtle secrets of divine life and living can be implemented. An intensification of practice will naturally ensue, but not until clarity is gained. To intensify an impure and unprepared mind is inadvisable. Using another analogy, it is rather like attempting to pray before one draws close to God through deep meditation and communion, i.e., either nothing will transpire, or negative propensities in the mind will get accented. Religion, or rather what Vivekananda called "*irreligion*," is famous for such misguided proceedings.

After receiving a clean bill of health, and with one's spiritual pulse beating steady and strong, the qualified disciple can both move forward and grow in spirituality, and effectively pass the teachings of the *dharma* on to others — making sure to advise a daily visit to the doctor's office of *guru*/disciple relationship to all who would seek the Goal of human existence. As the Great Master and World Teacher, Sri Ramakrishna, has stated:

"*Conducting life and spiritual growth in the right spirit gets rid of impurities in the mind like good medicine rids one of diseases. The mind then becomes like fertile soil free of rocks and roots, and seeds that are sown there will grow well.*"

Om Peace, Peace, Peace!

Pure Pretense
Talk is So Cheap that Even Children Can Buy It

A worldly person's talk of God is all pretense, and is most often based upon mere hearsay gotten from some unreliable or questionable source or sources. Even within the confines of a church or temple, most people's thoughts are continually fixed on matters of work, business, and profit, and their talk can even fall to the base level of gossip and slander. In short, living beings do not know how to strike up an atmosphere of sanctity and maintain it, even for a few minutes.

As a result, back home, the tone and tenor of daily communications follow suit, and words like "damn," "bless," "oath," "swear," and particularly "God," etc., are tossed around in conversation lightly and blithely. Little ears pick up such words and expressions and adopt them, trying them out with their friends while they are at play. "I swear to God that I did not cheat," or "May I be damned if this is not true," etc., easily and innocently come forth from small mouths in the name of impressing friends. This was seen and heard by Sri Ramakrishna as well, so he said: "When children play, they sometimes swear by God when they want their playmates to believe them. Perhaps they have heard their elders doing the same in their chatty conversations."

Sacredness in thought, word, and deed is a rare and precious thing. Meditation, silence, and non-agency underlie each, respectively. To quiet mind, mouth, and movement, when practiced consciously, ushers in a sense of the sacred which then permeates everything. Frequenting holy company, study of scripture, and *mantra* recitation fill in the rest, and enlightenment dawns in stages. Vasishtha teaches this silent *yoga* in no uncertain terms:

Sri Ram: "*Revered sir, how can silence, the mere stoppage of the lips from speaking words, conduce to realization?*"

Lord Vasishtha: "*True mauna, silence, is not measured or defined* by non-verbalization only. First and foremost, silence in regard to material pleasures is enjoined. When the desire for objects is stilled, then the mind has at least a chance to meditate properly and traditionally, approaching the state of Yoga. Further, when the inner chatter of the mind and senses are stilled, words, both internal and external, will be replaced by one sound and one sound only, by the supreme Word – Aum. And beyond this, when silence of intellect and ego is gained, The Great Silence, called Atman, will be enjoyed. Mauna at three levels, then, all three beyond a mere giving up of words, is to be contemplated, attained, and observed."

Limitless Luminosity
Out, Damn Spot! Well....Never Mind

About human imperfections, Sri Ramakrishna has used a simple illustration to shed (moon) light on the matter, saying: *"Dark spots are seen on the moon's surface, but they do not block out its luminous light."* In other words, there are imperfections in human nature by design, and even great souls may retain small defects thereby. But in their case there is no loss of effectivity. It is as if when darkness abides in them, the light shines all the more brightly from all other areas of their being. Further, where shadows reside in them, they are merely thin veils that can be easily lifted off when the Mother of their souls deems it timely.

Additionally, these tiny imperfections help to keep these illumined ones in the body so as to accomplish their mission and divine works. They will also use such "dark spots" on the moon of *manas* (dual mind) to help them identify with suffering souls in order to lift them up and out of darkness, *maya's* veils.

Such darkness can also work in reverse in the case of a spiritually awakened soul, acting to attract benighted souls by way of empathy and commiseration. As the Great Master has stated, *"A wretched hemp smoker loves the company of another addict, no matter how pathetic and degraded such a one has become, but if he sees a clean and finely dressed prince coming towards him, he will run away in haste."* You see, he is in sympathy with one of his own kind, since they share the error of their ways. To look into Holy Mother's experience with the moon and its halcyon light:

*"I have done much more than necessary in order
to make my life a model.
Ah, the ecstasy of those days!
On moonlit nights I would look at the moon
and pray with folded hands,
'May my heart be as pure as the rays of yonder moon!' or,
'Lord, there is a stain even in the moon,
but let there not be the least trace of stain in my mind.'"*

A Truly Divine Inheritance
Bourne on the Wings of Love

When love of God takes precedence over all other considerations and a man can think of nothing else, then the Lord Himself comes forward to take care of family and the affairs of the world. This is the gist of what Sri Ramakrishna means to say, using the following story of a young boy whose father has passed away: *"The under-aged son of a deceased landlord is taken under wing by a court-appointed guardian until he is of age and able to work and handle financial matters."*

Ideally, people who seek God rather than "Mammon" all receive His grace in the form of this timely protection from the world while they adjust to the subtleties and differences of new life lived in the Divine. This observance of the Great Master suggests a transitional period wherein the responsibilities of both the soul and his or her loved ones, as well as all their earthly affairs, get assumed by a higher power. Though quite amazing, and initially unbelievable, this Divine "takeover" is a proven fact of spiritual aspiration, practice, and consummation as experienced by so many sincerely-seeking souls whose time in the cycle of time on the not-so-fun merry-go-round of relativity has finally come to an end.

Further proof of this subtle fact is to be found in the mass of unfortunate cases of embodied beings whose earthly duties, activities, and responsibilities spiral out of control, descending into that dreadful old dive of *karmic* debt and despondency which awaits all beings dwelling unknowingly in *samsara*, devoid of the protective arms of the Universal Mother's Divine Love. To quote India's poet/saints and seers, again:

*"O Goddess, Your terrible garland of severed heads
inspires complete renunciation of birth and death, concept,
and convention – this Divine Drama that You demonstrate clearly
to be Your own magical display.
You have taught me to address Your awesome Reality
with the most tender name, and have awakened
the Divine Madness of Love so I am constantly weeping
'Mother, Mother, Mother.'
Where did You get a name so sweet, so replete with
the nectar of timeless bliss?
Citizens of the mundane realm address me as the
crazy poet of the Mother.
Members of my own family deride me.
But would I stray from your Path because of worldly abuse,
dearest Mother?
Let limited minds make any judgment they wish;
I will always continue to sing Kali, Kali, Kali.
Conventional honor and dishonor are equal to me.
I have turned away from Mother's shadow play,
and made Her delicate red-soled Feet,
Her dynamic Wisdom Essence, the meaning and goal
of my existence.
I can no longer even hear the misguiding chatter
of the world."*

— *For more Godblogs go to community.srvwisdom.org*

Rabbi Rami Shapiro ◆

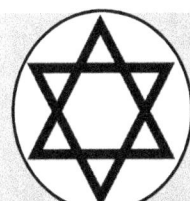

SEEING THE FACE OF GOD
Breaking Through the Prison of Narrow Mind

Call it what you will — the *Kali Yuga*, the Sixth Extinction, the Dark Night of the Soul, the Crucifixion of Human Civilization — we are in the midst of a cataclysmic moment where the destruction of millions of beings from drought, famine, flood, fire, hurricanes, tsunamis, pandemics, rising seas, collapsing liberal democracies, rising fascist autocracies, racism, antisemitism, genocide, and war is inevitable. Anyone who still asks how we might avoid this is not paying attention. The only question left to ask is how we might mitigate the hell we are bringing upon the world.

The key to mitigation is to grasp what is causing this madness and then do what we can to free ourselves from it. The cause is what Albert Einstein called humanity's optical delusion of consciousness:

A human being is part of a whole, called by us the "Universe," a part limited in time and space. We experience ourselves, our thoughts and feelings, as something separated from the rest — a kind of optical delusion of our consciousness. This delusion is a kind of prison for us, restricting us to our personal desires and to affection for a few persons nearest us. Our task must be to free ourselves from this prison by widening our circles of compassion to embrace all living creatures and the whole of nature in its beauty.

Einstein is a Jew, and while you might not know it from the statement just cited, he is speaking from the deepest spiritual insight of Judaism. To see how this is so and to discover how we might fulfill the task (the Hebrew word is *tikkun*/to heal) he sets before us, let me "translate" Einstein back into his Jewish roots.

The Whole Einstein refers to is God: not the anthropomorphic tribal God of the Jews, but the nondual God whose ineffable name *Yod Hay Vav Hay* is a form of the Hebrew verb "to be." *Yod Hay Vav Hay* isn't a being or even a Supreme Being but be/ing itself. As the 16th Century *Kabbalist* Moshe Cordovero wrote, "YHVH (Yod Hay Vav Hay) is found in all things and all things are found in YHVH... Everything is in YHVH is in everything and beyond everything, and there is nothing other than YHVH."

The self that experiences itself as separate from others is *mochin d'katnut*, narrow mind, and is trapped in dualistic consciousness and engages life from the zero-sum perspective of us against them and winner takes all. This is the self *Torah* reveals in the first chapter of Genesis where God (in this story called *Elohim*) says, "*Let us create humanity in our image after our likeness*" (Genesis 1:26).

Unlike in the following chapter where the earthling (*adam* in Hebrew) comes directly from the earth (*adamah*), humanity in this chapter is alien to and alienated from nature: there is no natural role for humans to play in nature. Instead, the authors of this story imagine the only role they could for these aliens: to rule over nature which in and of itself needs no ruler. God says to the humans: "*Be fruitful and multiply and fill the earth and subdue it and have dominion over the fish of the sea and over the birds of the air and over every living thing that moves upon the earth*" (Genesis 1:28). It is this alien and alienating fantasy of human domination that defines narrow mind and, I suggest, feeds the delusion of dualistic consciousness at its core. Thankfully, it is not the only option we have in the Hebrew Bible.

The self that breaks through the prison of narrow mind is *mochin d'gadlut*, spacious mind. Spacious mind sees through the delusion of othering and engages life from a nondual, nonzero perspective of all of us together where no one wins unless all of us win. This is the self *Torah* reveals in the second chapter of Genesis.

> "The self that breaks through the prison of narrow mind is *mochin d'gadlut*, spacious mind. Spacious mind sees through the delusion of othering and engages life from a nondual, nonzero perspective of all of us together where no one wins unless all of us win."

In this story, the earth is barren because it lacks two things essential to its thriving: water and a caretaker devoted to cultivating life. God (in this story called *Yod Hay Vav Hay*) brings forth water from the ground, and then fashions an earthling from the now damp and malleable earth. *Yod Hay Vav Hay* breathes consciousness into the earthling and gives it a very different mission than that articulated in Genesis 1: not to dominate and rule over life, but to "serve and protect" life (Genesis 2:15).

The task of spacious mind is made all the more important when you know that the Hebrew word *avodah*, "to serve," is the same word used for "worship": to serve life is an act of worship, an act of sacred service or what Genesis later calls "*being a blessing to all the families of the earth*" (Genesis 12:3). You are a blessing when you take upon yourself the task of freeing ourselves from the prison of narrow mind to the liberation of spacious mind is the work of *lech lecha* (journeying from self to Self). This task is the pri-

> "When you see the face of another being, human and otherwise,
> you feel inwardly commanded to treat that being with justice, compassion, and love.
> This is so because seeing the face of another is seeing the Face of God,
> the Face of *Yod Hay Vav Hay*."

mal call of *Yod Hay Vav Hay*:

"*Lech lecha* from your country, your kin and your parents home to the place I will show you. In this way, you will...be a blessing to all the families of the earth." (Genesis 12:1, 3).

Yod Hay Vav Hay, be/ing itself, calls to you saying *Lech lecha* from your country and your kin and your parents to the place I will show you. *Lech* means to "walk" or "journey." *Lecha* means "toward your Self." *Lech lecha* is an inner journey of liberation from narrow mind and the conditioning of nationality, ethnicity, religion, race, gender, etc. to a place that I [*Yod Hay Vav Hay*] will show you.

What is this place? It is a place of liberation where you are not bound by labels. Notice that lech lecha is a journey without a map. It is the way of *neti-neti* and *via negativa*. You don't arrive at a specific location, but at a state of mind where you are a "blessing to all the families of the earth." *Lech lecha* is the task that all humans must make if we are, as Einstein said, to "*free ourselves from this prison [of dualism] by widening our circles of compassion to embrace all living creatures and the whole of nature in its beauty.*"

There are many ways to do this in Judaism. I will focus on only one: the practice of *Shiviti*.

In the mid-twentieth century the French Jewish philosopher Emmanuel Levinas taught what is called an ethic of the face: when you see the face of another being, human and otherwise, you feel inwardly commanded to treat that being with justice, compassion, and love. This is so because seeing the face of another is seeing the Face of God, the Face of *Yod Hay Vav Hay*.

Remember *Yod Hay Vav Hay* isn't a being but be/ing itself. The 18th century Hasidic Rebbe Menachum Nachum Twersky called *Yod Hay Vav Hay Chiut* or Aliveness. Each life is an expression of Aliveness the way each wave is an expression of the ocean that waves it. To see any wave is the "face" of the ocean. Similarly, to see the face of every being is to the Face of Being itself.

Whenever I present this notion, some people resist it pointing to Exodus 33:20 where God says to Moses "*You cannot see My Face, for no one can see My Face and live.*" I counter with Psalm 27 where God says, "*Seek My Face!*" (Psalm 27:8). Reading these two texts together from the perspective of spacious mind, I find no conflict at all:

God says, "*Seek My Face in every face, and when you see My Face as every face you cannot live as you did before you saw My Face. Before you saw My Face you felt free to have dominion over the other, but after you see My Face, you can only engage the other with compassion and justice.*"

Seeing the face of the other as other, is the seeing of narrow mind. Seeing the face of the other as the Face of God is the seeing of spacious mind. Moving from narrow mind to spacious mind is the task of *lech lecha*. One way to do this is the precious practice of Shiviti.

The word *shiviti* means "I place" and comes with the practice is from Psalm 16:8: *shiviti YHVH (Yod Hay Vav Hay) l'negdi tamid*: "*I place the Divine before me always.*" The practice is to recite this verse whenever you draw near to the face of another being as a way of shifting from narrow to spacious mind and seeing the face of the other as the Face of God.

Since the Name of God, *YHVH*, is literally unpronounceable (being comprised of four consonants and no vowels), the ancient rabbis offered euphemisms to say in its place. The one I use here is *Shekhinah*, a feminine gendered word meaning the Presence of God. I recite the mantra this way: *shiviti Shekhinah l'negdi tamid (she-vee-tee sheh-khee-nah le neg-dee tah-meed)*.

The verse, however, speaks of placing. How do we move from placing to seeing?

The Dynamics of Shviti Practice

When reciting *shiviti* you consciously place the lens of *mochin d'gadlut* (spacious mind) in place of the lens of *mochin d'katnut* (narrow mind) and in this way you see the Face of God as every face. Not in the face of the other or on the face of the other, but as the face of the other. Whenever you see another—a human, an animal, a tree, etc., say to yourself *shiviti Shekhinah l'negdi tamid*; in time you will come to see the other as the One, and engage with the other in a manner aligned with "*being a blessing to all the families of the earth*" human and otherwise. What starts out as an act of will, in time becomes an act of grace. While the specifics of being a blessing change from encounter to encounter, the practice of *shiviti* makes each encounter a holy opportunity to, as Einstein put it, "*free ourselves from this prison by widening our circles of compassion to embrace all living creatures and the whole of nature in its beauty.*"

Rabbi Rami Shapiro is an award–winning author of over thirty-six books on religion and spirituality. He received rabbinical ordination from the Hebrew Union College–Jewish Institute of Religion and holds a PH.D. in religion from Union Graduate School. Rami co-directs the One River Foundation(www.oneriverfoundation.org), is a Contributing Editor at Spirituality and Health magazine where he writes the Roadside Assistance for the Spiritual Traveler column and hosts the magazine's podcast, Spirituality & Health with Rabbi Rami (www.spiritualityhealth.com).

Alexander Hixon ♦

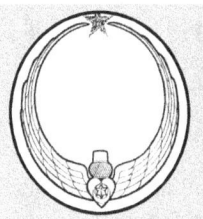

AN INTERVIEW WITH PIR VILAYET KHAN

This program on Pir Vilayet Khan is one of three existing interviews with the Sufi leader conducted by Lex Hixon on "In The Spirit," live over the air on WBAI radio in New York City in the 1980's.

This is the third program of a series on Islam — its mystical aspects and its orthodox aspects — since I myself have recently returned from Istanbul. Today we are going to be speaking with Pir Vilayet Khan. And this is a further departure from orthodox Islam, because Pir Vilayet Khan, as you may know, was born in the West of an American mother and an Indian Muslim father. He had the full mystical training of Islam, and yet he was educated at Oxford, and at other Western institutions, so that what we have in him is a very interesting mixture of East and West. And particularly now that he is interested in science, and what he calls the co-evolution of science and spirit, he makes some very interesting remarks: that he feels like he is a member of all religions, yet also thinks that the traditional forms of religion are beginning to pass away and other paths are emerging.

Lex Hixon: Pir Vilayet, I came not just to interview you, but to seek guidance from you. We have been laughing, and you have put us all at ease; maybe that is a part of the guidance, that I should not be so serious about certain things. But I have just spent a month in Istanbul living with an orthodox *dervish* community, and I had a very, very overwhelming experience of the power of Islam, and the power of the argument of Islam which includes living a life based upon the dedicated life that the Prophet lived — the five times a day prayer, the ablutions, and the ways that he lived. The impression that I received there was that the mystical life of Islam that we all feel so drawn to, and that we think of as Sufism, is not really easily separable from the life or orthodox Islam. I was overwhelmed by this feeling, and as I began practicing the orthodoxy in the environment there it felt very good, and very inspiring.

But at a certain point I realized that with contemporary Americans, like myself, that I could not fully embrace orthodox Islam; my sympathys go to a broader scope of all the world religions. So one of the first things that I wanted to do coming back to this country is to come to you, for after all your father was a member of the Chisti Order of India, and perhaps he also practiced the five times a day prayers, and yet you with an American mother and a liberal, humanistic Western education have not opted to teach the traditional way of Islam. So maybe you could advise me on this matter, and my problem.

Pir Vilayet Khan: Well, I can give you my opinion, but I would not assume to guide you on the subject, because this is a matter of conscience and everyone must decide for themselves how they feel most comfortable. I think you hit the nail on the head when you found it very comfortable to adopt the rituals of Islam when you were moving in that environment, and were in harmony with it. When you looked back upon it in retrospect, however, you felt that you could not continue the same practices in this environment. That's very very difficult, because I feel that the religions have developed in the course of civilizations very much like the plants developed in the course of evolution, or different species of animals. They all have that part to play in the whole. In a particular climate and a particular environment if you try to acclimatize it somewhere else, you may run into difficulties.

Lex Hixon: But Pir Vilayet, and excuse me for breaking in, but the fact is that we can and do plant plants from one country to another, and they grow essentially in the same way. For instance, your background and your father's was of an orthodox nature, yet you moved all the way from Mecca to India, yet still retained such practices as the five times a day prayer.

Pir Vilayet Khan: Yes, I think one can be more specific, for though we do transplant plants, science is finding out that they undergo some kind of mutation in order to adapt properly.

Now, there has always been in the past a dichotomy between those who observe the external forms of religion, and the mystic, who basically deconforms to the religious background in which they form, and they nevertheless have their roots in the tradition but grow their branches in further dimensions. In some extreme cases, of course, faced with the tradition, there are cases of some practitioners even been decapitated by the Emperor for their views. Many of the Sufis, anyway, have made statements that have offended the orthodoxy. Ignonamy, for instance, when he said that he is neither a Christian, nor a Jew, nor a Muslim, because he belongs to the religion of Love, offended the orthodoxy. I wouldn't declare that; I would say that I am a Muslim, and a Christian, and a Jew, and a Hindu. I don't accept the way he is talking. I think that it is more a matter of what Hazrat Inayet Khan calls, "The Message of our Time." In fact, he puts it well: he says, "There is only the breech between the followers of the Prophet, and the followers of the followers of the Prophet. The prophet was giving the message of his time to a people who — to whom he gave a new impulse by the very severity of the discipline that he imposed, gave them a rule of life that was absolutely indispensible in order to bring about the growth of a new civilization.

They say in Islam that the new Islam is in exile, referring, of course, to what happened to the Prophet, but they mean by that, that behind the outer form, which is what most people are able to appreciate, there is a deeper aspect of Islam which is the mystical side. That is beyond the formalism of the Sheriyat.

Lex Hixon: But strangely enough, in the community where I was, in Istanbul, there was a tremendously deep harmony between the

Sheriyat and the mystical side; they were so deeply intertwined that even the Sheriyat became the mystical. The Shiekh who leads that community does not simply go through the motions of the daily prayer and the various formal aspects of Islam, but he does it with such joy and ecstasy that it doesn't make any sense to call it the outer mechanical form anymore.

Pir Vilayet Khan: No, of course not. It's an expression of an inner experience,, and that makes it very beautiful. Actually, Hazrat Inayet Khan, my father, said, "There is not one drop of blood in my veins that is not Muslim. If you look in the deep recesses of Hazrat Inayet Khan's teachings, you will find the deep mysticism behind the external signs. But as I said, most people only follow the external do's and don'ts without understanding the real depths of Islam.

Lex Hixon: If someone were to ask you, for instance, how much you feel that you are a Muslim, you are a Christian, you are a Buddhist and a Hindu, would you say that you are more a Muslim than the others? Do you feel some sort of basic root there, since your father, who was your teacher and the leader of the order, said there was not a drop of blood in him that was not Muslim....how would you respond?

Pir Vilayet Khan: I would say that I feel myself not apt to make any comparisons between the religions, being not qualified to. You are asking me as well a personal question too, and I could say that when I am amongst the very deep mystical side of Islam, there is a certain quality there that I can't easily define....it is quite holy.

Lex Hixon: Since I came back from Istanbul I understand much more and more. That is what I feel is outlined very strongly in Hazrat Inayet Khan's teaching, an accent on the import of what is achieved in the world, whereas the Hindu and Buddhist teachings were very much oriented towards the *nirvana* and *samadhi* states which is beyond life, and transcendental. That's where Hazrat Inayet Khan says it in the way that is most meaningful to me, when he speaks about experiencing the divine Consciousness or breaking into the divine Mind and experiencing conditions from within the creation. Homage can be offered to *samadhi* when you reach the illumined state before creation, so it doesn't prevent me from appreciating what Buddhism has to teach. One can experience the beauties of life and at the same time experience detachment. I like very much the teaching that one can look upon one's body, one's mind, and even one's consciousness without identifying with it. That is a special contribution of Buddhism, and Hinduism before it.

There is a saying in France, that a child might feel that his mother is the most beautiful woman in the world, but when he grows up he realizes that there are many beautiful women in the world, and he is not being untrue to his mother by finding this out. So, I think that we should appreciate what all the religions have to teach.

Lex Hixon: I am very happy to hear these words, because I myself have been drawn to accept the various religious traditions, and not simply study them from the outside, but somehow merge with them in a real way. But my faith was shaken when I was in Istanbul this summer, when I saw that perhaps one really had to be rooted

> "There is a saying in France, that a child might feel that his mother is the most beautiful woman in the world, but when he grows up he realizes that there are many beautiful women in the world, and he is not being untrue to his mother by finding this out. So, in this way, I think that we should appreciate what all the religions have to teach."

more how Islam spread to India. It has an inner conquering force which is not related at all to military victories. It possess a flavor of conquering, but it conquers one's heart, one's spirit. I felt myself being profoundly absorbed in it in just the brief time I was there.

Pir Vilayet Khan: For me, of course, the door to Islam is the mystical experience of the Sufis. Al-Hallaj, for example, said that his own understanding has been entirely shattered by the Divine understanding; that is something that is very meaningful for me. For instance, I see fellow teachers of other religions trying to express Truth via rational thinking, and here is someone who realizes the total inadequacy of rational thinking. I realize, then, that in Islam there is a hint of the seeds of the trend which would nowadays be called holistic. A lot of Muslims think that they are being untrue to their prophet if they speak about the unity of all the prophets, and yet it is right there in the Koran.

Lex Hixon: Also, in the Koran, the tremendous feeling for the creation and its essential unity; that's a wonderful basis for science.

Pir Vilayet Khan: And that's the thing that I feel is underlying in a single tradition in order to really realize and express it authentically. You mention knowing about many beautiful women, but really, it is through marriage that one really realizes the unity and deep feeling of love.

Pir Vilayet Khan: I have often found that people who are too eclectic lose their sense of loyalty, and I have sometimes found mystics who might be said to be too narrow minded. I once heard that some of the statements of St. Francis were anti-heathen, or anti-Islamic, and I once consulted a Mushadin in Hyderabad for whom the only way was Islam, and declared that all other religions are quite on the wrong path. So it is curious that people who I would quite seriously consider narrow-minded could, on the other hand, display very deep mystical attainment. So, I would say, that some people could reach the top of the mountain better when they are following a very defined path. But I, myself, would sometimes like to leave the garden paths and go through the bush, the brush, and reach the top using paths that are not so well defined.

Lex Hixon: I wonder how many....I myself have met a few people who I would consider as living saints, Mother Teresa of Kolkata,

> "....sometimes there are only a few minds on the planet that are able to see the next step; the others are way back in the past, and the former are supposed to be pioneers while other people follow. When one studies so deeply, then see to what extent the wholistic approach conforms exactly to all the things that my father, Hazrat Inayet Khan, said, quite a long time ago, that is far-sighted."

for instance. I briefly touched on the subject of the harmony of all religions with her, and realized immediately that that was not something that she would necessarily understand, or sympathize with. For her, her Christ is the way, but her Christ is a very compassionate and vast heart who somehow mysteriously embraces Muslim and Hindus and Buddhists also. A person as vast as her certainly cannot be exclusive in any way.

Pir Vilayet Khan: Yes, of course, the heart of humanity, or one can even say the heart of God, well, she speaks in terms of her religious background. That is exactly what I am saying, that the people that you meet in the course of your visits or your pilgrimages are always talking in terms of their backgrounds. And that is the point you just made when you said that you felt perfectly at home in that practice of Islam and five times a day prayers, then you came home to a different environment, and it also has its favorable points. Therefore, one can follow a narrow path, but those who feel that the time is coming when the path will be converging or uniting, those are the people who are working towards the unity of all religions.

Lex Hixon: One of the interesting things is to become aware of what really is one's background. For instance, in our culture here in the West, what is our background, which we may not really be aware of, is imbuing the culture in many subtle ways, but we may think that it is just the ordinary way of looking at things. It would include science and humanism, and various forms of Christian and Jewish thinking. So, possibly, over here, we have a very strong background which we are not really that aware of. It is informing us all of the time.

Pir Vilayet Khan: You know, Hazrat Inayet Khan was so very deeply impressed about what he encountered here in America, and of course in Europe. It was a bit of a culture shock, of course, at first, but later on he got in touch with some of the leading industrialists of his time who were idealists. Then he said himself that he wondered if some of the *rishis* in the Himalayas would be so selfless as these beings who were promoting the welfare of the workers in their factorys. I once met a man living in a tiny room, and he had something like 8000 people working for him. He was giving them work, and striving to help their social well-being, and so forth. So what I am saying is that there is so much conformism to patterns sometimes, like in the *ashrams* of the East. In the West there seems to be a sense of authenticity in spiritual matters, and very much concern about them. And another thing, I felt that there was a lot of superstition there, whereas the European and the American way is more of a realistic look at things.

Lex Hixon: And that is based on the long and painful struggle that came about through the reformation, and the introduction of Science, and even industrialization, so in a certain sense our Western viewpoint is a result of a great deal of sacrifice on the part of dedicated people. It's not just something like a materialism, or secularism.

About background, Pir Vilayet, one thing that returned to when I came back to this country, and being very disoriented, was my original spiritual teachings that I, so to speak, grew up with. I was an agnostic as a child. My parents were not a member of any church. In my early twenties I met Swami Nikhilananda of the Ramakrishna Order and spent seven years with him studying the Vedanta and meditating on Ramakrishna who was an all-embracing being, you might say, a real Sufi. So I returned to this and thought, for some strange reason, perhaps this is my background, and that perhaps I am really rooted in that particular tradition and I am seeing all the other traditions in the light of that. And I wonder, in your case, perhaps you are really rooted in the teachings of your father, Inayet Khan, and that you are seeing everything else in the light of that. In that sense you could say, you are not eclectic at all; you are really singularly focused.

Pir Vilayet Khan: That is true. But I think the reason is, not because he happens to be my father, but because that teaching is so much in tune with the teaching of the planet. And what is more, sometimes there are only a few minds on the planet that are able to see the next step; the others are way back in the past, and the former are supposed to be pioneers while other people follow. When one studies so deeply, then to see to what extent the wholistic approach confirms exactly all the things that my father, Hazrat Inayet Khan said, quite a long time ago, that is far-sighted.

For example, up to the present, they thought that the cells of the body were homeostatic, meaning they seek to maintain a certain balance. But now it is found that they are always heliostatic, which means that they are always striving to improve their condition. Now, with my father, one of the things that struck me is that his teachings were always purpose-oriented, goal-oriented, whereas the teachings of the past were very cause-oriented — like Buddhism, always trying to find the cause behind the cause behind the cause, and explaining things in terms of *karma* and then *samadhi*, where there is no condition before the creation — whereas his teachings absolutely accent the insight of what is actually being fulfilled on the planet at the particular moment.

And I think, that quite clearly we must move forward, that the whole purpose of our lives is to keep breaking through to new horizons; the whole of evolution is just exactly that. And that is why I am talking about adherence or conformism to patterns. I think that those patterns are a sclerosis of an inspiration. As Hazrat Inayet Khan says, the laws, and even the laws of nature are what have constricted what could otherwise have been a divine, free act. Of course, it is natural that people feel more secure when they are conformed to patterns; that's the basis of religion. But at the height of religion there is always the deeper import and ecstasy.

Lex Hixon: Excuse me, but returning once more to causes, one more time. I know that there is quite an interesting similarity between Swami Vivekananda and Hazrat Inayet Khan. Vivekananda came to the United States for the first time in 1883 for the Parliament of Religions. Hazrat came early in the 1900's...about 1910, so they really were contemporaries. Just possibly, since Vivekananda had received such wide publicity in India, your father may have heard about this trip. [both laugh]

Pir Vilayet Khan: Well, my father gave me a picture of Sri Ramakrishna to put up on my wall! And then, Swami Siddeshwarananda of the Ramakrishna Mission in Paris, who had such tremendous success there, visited the house of my father there in Paris. And he was at that time giving a lecture. There were two plates, two brass plates on the mantle, and as soon as he spoke about the link between Hazrat Khan and Sri Ramakrishna, all of a sudden they moved to face each other. And when he invited me to speak at his center in Gretz, at the very moment I spoke about their relationship, again two things in the room moved to face each other. [laughter]

Lex Hixon: Minds and hearts touch each other at these times, Pir Vilayet. I've always felt that Hazrat Inayet and Ramakrishna, as well as Vivekananda who came here as a young man following a visionary path, knew that there is something here in the West more than just materialism and affluence, that there was a potentiality here.

Pir Vilayet Khan: You see, the interesting thing was, that here was someone coming from the Hindu tradition into this religious attitude, and someone from the Muslim tradition coming as well, to meet; it is so meaningful and a prime example of what is happening on the planet at this time.

Lex Hixon: It seems possible that this kind of harmony of religions may not have been able to arrive from anywhere other than India.

Pir Vilayet Khan: This is also what I was thinking. You see, you have spent some time in Turkey, and I know a few people who have gone to visit the Sufis in North Africa. You must understand that in those countries, the official religion is Islam. Now if you go to India you find a totally different climate. You find that the Hindus and the Muslims have lived together for decades and even centuries, and in fact, that it was only political propaganda that divided them. My great grandfather had two wives, one Hindu and one Muslim, and there was a lot of intermingling between Hindus and Muslims; and even if there wasn't, they were always friends. As you know, there were so many mystics who tried to find equal measure between the two. Some of them were so grounded in both, that it was almost impossible to determine whether they were Hindu or Muslim. There was a certain story that when a certain one of those mystics started to pass away, both his Hindu followers and his Muslim followers came to claim his remains, and he ended up jumping over his coffin and running into the woods so that he could die in peace. [laughter].

Lex Hixon: Pir Vilayet: When you pass away do you want to be buried or cremated?

Pir Vilayet Khan: I want to offer my body to a hospital for scientific experiments. [laughter]

Lex Hixon: [laughing] That's wonderful A totally Western development. My mind goes back to India to a climate that can create the possibility of this kind of fusion of religions. One thing I have learned by knowing Islam more intimately, is how deeply Indian culture is permeated by Islam, so that there is really so much in what I thought was Hinduism before that is Islamic. After all, it was there for some 800 years or so before the British came. There was a tremendous interpenetration.

Pir Vilayet Khan: Yes, and it is there even in the architecture as well. But I think that it is also true that there was a kind of harmonious cohabitation of Hindus and Muslims, and it has saved people from being attached to their forms.

Lex Hixon: Do you think that this should be kept up, and do you think that there should be people who do keep independent traditions of Christianity and Judaism, and Islam, or do you think that gradually those things will fall away.

Pir Vilayet Khan: Yes. They are eventually going to fall away....

Lex Hixon: Are they?! These religious traditions are much deeper than just clothes or costumes and customs.

Pir Vilayet Khan: Of course; they are much deeper. But I think there will be more and more forms emerging. That is absolutely certain, though it may take a long time.

Lex Hixon: I would say that there is a clear point of disagreement between us here. I would look to the fact of these independent religions are existing always in their own purity, kept up by people who have that kind of destiny.

Pir Vilayet Khan: That's very beautiful, what you say. I certainly would not encourage people to leave their religion and experience all kinds of new religions, or a new synthetic kind of religion, no, but I think that it's bound to happen.

Lex Hixon: I see. Pir Vilayet, let's talk about the Abode of the Message, where you have founded the home of this Order. Is this message the message of Hazrat Inayet Khan, your father, or of the Prophet? What message is this the abode of? I mean, it could be the abode of the message of our time, and not one of just the past.

Pir Vilayet Khan: Yes, but both are one message that comes down; it is the same message as ever.

Lex Hixon: It's one message that always comes down?

Pir Vilayet Khan: Yes.

Lex Hixon: [laughing] I like that. I want to switch gears in our conversation now, and speak about the symposium on the co-evolution of science and spirit that is being sponsored by the Sufi Order in the West. This is the direction, apparently, that the message is going at this point. Perhaps you could say something about it?

Pir Vilayet Khan: There is no doubt that one is driven by one's own idiosyncrasies, hopefully with overall guidance in the background, of course. It wasn't incidental that I studied science in college when I was a young one, but it was there in my mind, so this particular subject is important to me at this time. Because I think we are passing through a real gridlock in the evolution of human consciousness at this time, or at least prefiguring what will be a landmark in the year 2000, and I think that the actual thought on the whole thing is to become the word, hologram. It is something that the people are just beginning to discover, called the holistic approach. What does it mean? It derives from the word wholeness, but also from the word holy, and even the word health. In all religions it is a very significant word. The starting point is discovering that a crystal is made of molecules, and if you break it up into many pieces, you will find that every fragment behaves just like the entire crystal. What this really means, is that if you extend this concept to man, that man is not only a fragment of the totality, but also epitomizes the characteristics of the totality. And if you extend this experiment into religion, you could say that man is not only a fragment of the being of God, he has also within him the divine perfection of God.

And this is exactly what Inayet Khan said when he was asked what is the message of our time, and he said, "It is the awakening of the consciousness of the divinity in man." In other words, we have reached the point where we cannot simply go on thinking of ourselves as a separate entity and a fragment of the totality, limited by "I-ness," but we have to be aware of the eternal, undying dimension of our being. That's the wholistic message of our time.

Scientists are beginning to realize that these limitations of the past — although it was true that they believed that what they discovered before was absolutely true — that now they are not trued any longer. So at present, the scientists are not at all convinced and have not seen the confusion that the intellectual perspective has brought about.

Lex Hixon: But I wonder that if one finds a scientist who already has a predilection of being a visionary, and therefore cuts through all the middle range of science, to use your term — which is a very important stage of science that many beings never get through — and gets to the upper edge of science and gets to look over the horizon, and feels this awe, and maybe has certain perceptions, isn't there a long way still from there to achieve sainthood?

Pir Vilayet Khan: Well, its very difficult to follow one's way to the goal of the spiritual path, and at the same time involve oneself in everyday activities, and that might also pertain to the scientist too. Its a gradual process, of course, but I would never like to admit that it's impossible. I do think it's a bit easier if you are wearing the world, just to sit in the corner and show compassion to the people, then when you have people stepping on your toes, pushing you aside, and insulting you. Its much easier to have this aura of sanctity and be considered with very much respect. But the test is to go right into life and show the same respect when you are being challenged. If the scientist is able to maintain his spiritual ideal while dealing with matter, I think it's a great achievement.

Lex Hixon: What about the simple religious person — the simple Christian, the simple Muslim, who is really not so simple if they are a dedicated person, but I don't mean to suggest someone of tremendous sanctity, but a sincere follower of that particular spiritual path, say, grounded in the Koran or the Bible, grounded in the prayers, trying to open every moment to the blessings of God — it seems to me that this person has a much better chance for spiritual growth then the scientist or the intellectual who is floating out there in space, looking askance at all the religions....

Pir Vilayet Khan: Well, it is quite clear that religion is for the masses; it gives people guidelines, and most people need them.....

Lex Hixon: Pir Vilayet, forgive me for interrupting, but when you say that religion is for the masses, it sounds like you are citing something different from what I understand as religion. To me its the highest possibility that human beings have.

Pir Vilayet Khan: Let's say, the instructions that people get in their various religions are a little bit like the briefings that parents give to their children, like what not to do and so forth.

Lex Hixon: But what I mean is the deeper things about religion, like transmissions about attitudes, about faith, and harmony and order. I don't think you can reduce religion to simply rules about not doing.

Pir Vilayet Khan: Yes, but there is a big difference between the rules one follows in religion, and the mystic experience. That latter is the sacred part of the religion. But most people need some definite form to work with, and that's what the religions try to give, these religious institutions. There are those who can go into ecstasy rather easily, without having to attend mass, or prayers, or follow such rules, or can attend mass and experience that ecstasy as well. Then there are those who go to mass because if they are told to and if they don't go they will go to hell. [laughter]

Lex Hixon: I feel that you are making an argument by extremes, whereas there is a tremendous middle ground there as well.

Pir Vilayet Khan: Yes, I admit that. Let me give you an example, if there is time. When I used to organize a retreat at Easter in France, a very Catholic country, the people who came were Catholics, and they wished to go to midnight mass. One day they said to me, well, couldn't we just perform mass here. I was surprised, but we performed mass together. We broke bread and all. Then, at the end of the mass, everyone was absolutely transported. Now, that very morning we all had a meditation on Light. After the meditation, I looked up at the faces of the people and thought to myself, I can't seem to see any divinity shining in the faces of these people. What am I teaching meditation on Light for; what is the point of teaching that when it doesn't seem to have any effect on them? I felt a kind of collapse of all that I had tried to do. That evening, we had a ceremony, and everyone was transported. Then I realized that there is a purpose in all forms of practice.

So as I just said, I realize that there is a great efficacy in all these forms. What I am saying further is, as time goes on, people are giving up forms, although they have value. It is like, for example, people have given up what it takes to build a cathedral like Notre Dam, and they are building other churches. So within the Catholic tradition they are always changing their forms, and that's because, whereas the forms have their value, that value changes and they do have to change as a result.

Lex Hixon: And your Order, your Sufi Order of the West, while it accents the mystical side, it also has its forms in the way of its Universal Worship you composed, which involves using various symbols from the different religions together on the altar.

Pir Vilayet Khan: Well, I'll always accent both aspects.

Lex Hixon: Yes, I will too, and we can go on happily talking like this, about this, eternally. Thank you so much, Pir Vilayet......

◆ ANNAPURNA SARADA

ABSOLUTE REALITY & GOD
Qualification for Meditation

"He who understands the secret of the Personal Deity (being the manifestation of the Power of the Absolute) and has absorption in the Absolute simultaneously, attains the spiritual felicity of transcendence by absorption in the Absolute, having conquered the travails of life by devotion to the Personal God." - Isavasyopanisad, Swami Sarvananda, trans.

The *rishi* declares, above, that beings attain to the Absolute via devotion to the Personal God (*Ishvara*, in Sanskrit), who is a manifestation of the power of *Brahman*, all pervasive, formless Reality. Through this devotion, one conquers the problems of relative existence, for example: suffering, doubt, karma, fear, anger, pride, etc. This echoes the words of Jesus when he stated that no one gets to the Father except through Me (John, 14:6). This is a timely statement for the current religious and spiritual culture of the West influenced by teachings emphasizing nonduality or formlessness. Many, following the path of formless Reality, have a feeling of antipathy or resistance towards God with form, arising variously from narrow religious teachings, or the assumption that it is a mere imagination unrelated to the formless Absolute, or that devotion to *Ishvara* is a form of weakness and will keep one from attaining realization of the Absolute. In such cases practitioners conclude all forms must be set aside from the beginning. This is an unfortunate understanding, for it does not take into account the stages of understanding and capacity that beings progress through in spiritual life. The history of Indian religious and philosophical culture is an example of what happens for individual spiritual aspirants.

The ancient practitioners of India in their search for the ultimate cause of existence deified the cosmic forces they perceived, discovering both gross and subtle principles. Looking outward, they recognized five gross elements (earth, water, fire, air, ether), and in the body, the cognitive and active senses (hearing, seeing, tasting, etc., and handling, moving, speaking, etc.). Continuing ever more inwardly for the source of these elements and senses, they perceived the mind, subtle elements (*tanmatras*), ego, intellect, and the Cosmic Mind (each more subtle than the previous) as the next levels of cause. All these were deified, personified, and propitiated for earthly and heavenly harmony and well-being. By practicing sacrifices and worship to these elemental, psychical, and cosmic deities, combined with concentrated meditation, they honed and purified their minds. As the *Svetashwatara Upanisad* declared:

"Practicing the yoga of meditation, the seers beheld the Divine Being existing everywhere, and in everything, and which, though veiled by its own modes of nature (the Gunas), was nonetheless one and indivisible - and which had been imperceptible earlier due to the limitations of their own intellects."

These ancient ones thereby delivered to humanity an understanding of the Absolute and Relative, the Impersonal and Personal, Nondual Reality and the Divine Being of the Universe, through the process of concentrating on forms, from gross to subtle, until all forms melted away and the one Essence in all was revealed. Philosophically speaking, the rishis spoke of Brahman without attributes or qualities (*nirguna*) and Brahman with attributes (*saguna*). The Absolute is the former and the Personal God the latter. Over time, the cosmic principles came to be understood as under the control of the Trinity (*Brahma, Vishnu, Shiva*) responsible for the Projection, Sustenance, and Dissolution of the Universe over cycles in Eternity. More recently, these three are often taken as the powers of *Ishvara* or *Ishwari* (feminine), the Personal God/Divine Being who appears as the highest Ideal of any religion or spiritual practitioner.

The *rishis* were seeking the ultimate origin of everything – *"What is that one thing by knowing which all else is known?"* As Swami Vivekananda has said, this seems to have been a peculiar bent of the ancient *Vedic* mind. Of course, human beings from different regions of the world wondered who created the universe, the earth, seas, stars, plants, animals, and humans. But to surmise that by knowing that "one thing" all else would be known seems to be unique to India. By way of example the *Upanishads* say: by knowing clay, all items made of clay are known. By knowing gold, all objects made of gold are known. Similarly, by knowing this Ultimate Reality, everything else is known; for "*Brahmadvitiye*" Brahman is one without a second.

The philosophical schools of India developed ways of explaining the nature of Ultimate Reality and the Personal God and how these two are one Reality in essence, only viewed from a transcendent perspective or from the individual perception. The question naturally arises, how has the One become the many? The answers to this are varied and subtle, and express how the power inherent in Ultimate Reality (*Maya, Shakti, Avidya*, etc.) conceals *Brahman's* nature as indivisible Consciousness, which simultaneously makes possible the appearance of multiplicity, the projection of the universe. As the verse above explains, this Divine Being (formless Reality) exists everywhere and in everything but is not limited by forms. It always remains indivisible. As long as the meditator's intellect is not transcended, indivisible Reality is not perceived.

The Absolute, God, & the Individual Soul

Ultimate or Absolute Reality (*Brahman*) is often called *Sat-chit-ananda*, Existence-Awareness-Bliss. Each part of this name is its very nature. These are not attributes that can be separated from It, like a gold necklace can be removed from one's body. The seers tell us that *Brahman's* nature is Existence without nonexistence; unwavering Awareness/Consciousness; and Bliss without cessation. It transcends time, space, causation, names, and forms and is one without a second. It is nonduality itself (free of the pairs of opposites, life/death, pleasure/pain, form/formlessness, good/bad, etc.) and is thus described as having no name, attributes, or qualities. These descriptions are still inadequate. As Sri Ramakrishna has stated: *"Brahman is beyond vidya and avidya, knowledge and ignorance. It is beyond maya, the illusion of duality.... What Brahman is cannot be described. All things in the world – the Vedas, the Puranas, the Tantras, the six systems of philosophy – have been defiled, like food that has been touched by the tongue, for they have been read or uttered by the tongue. Only one thing has not been defiled, and that is*

Brahman. No one has ever been able to say what Brahman is." (Gospel of Sri Ramakrishna, p. 102)

Thus, Absolute Reality/*Nirguna Brahman* is realized by transcending the mind, intellect, and ego in the rare state of complete absorption (*nirvikalpa samadhi, nirvana*). The seers, illumined sages, mystics, and divine Incarnations have realized this Absolute Reality; therefore, we know about it. Otherwise, despite it being one's own essence, most beings would overlook it, as in the metaphor of the fish who did not believe in water; It is our existence. But even here, as Sri Ramakrishna describes above, no one can truly say what *Brahman* is. One can only point towards the Reality with words. Sri Ramakrishna gives an analogy for this: a salt doll wanted to measure the depth of the ocean in order to tell others about it, but as soon as he entered the ocean, he dissolved into it. To describe something, there needs to be a witness of it. But in this case, the witness merges into *Brahman*. Sri Ramakrishna tried to describe to his disciples what it was like to merge into *Brahman*, but in each attempt, he merged into it.

The Personal God (*Ishvara*) is that very *Brahman* seen through the veil of time, space, causation, name, and form (*Maya, Avidya*/Ignorance) and is the highest conception possible to the human mind. *Ishvara* is the repository of all powers such as omniscience, omnipotence, creation, sustenance, dissolution, and all blessed qualities. Swami Vivekananda, in his lectures on *Bhakti Yoga*, the path of devotion, summarizes *Ishvara* as the God of Love whom all devotees adore, pray to, and place their faith and trust in regardless of their religion, no matter what name they use for God. *"'From whom is the birth, continuation, and dissolution of the universe,' – He is Ishvara – 'the Eternal, the Pure, the Ever-Free, the Almighty, the All-Knowing, the All-Merciful, the Teacher of all teachers'; ... Are there then two Gods – the 'Not this, not this,' ...the Existence-Knowledge-Bliss of the philosopher, and this God of Love of the Bhakta [devotee]? No, it is the same Sat-chit-ananda who is also the God of Love, the impersonal and personal in one. It has always to be understood that the Personal God worshipped by the Bhakta is not separate or different from Brahman. All is Brahman, the One without a second; only Brahman, as unity or absolute, is too much of an abstraction to be loved and worshipped; so the Bhakta chooses the relative aspect of Brahman, that is, Ishvara, the Supreme Ruler.* (Complete Works of Swami Vivekananda (CW), vol 3, p. 37)

As for the individual soul, we learn in the *Upanisads* and other scriptures that *Brahman* is the Reality behind both *Ishvara* and the individual soul. Vedanta clarifies their distinction philosophically by explaining that *Brahman's* inherent Power that conceals *Brahman* and projects the universe has cosmic and individual aspects. *Ishvara* is *Brahman* appearing through cosmic ignorance/*maya*; and the individual soul (*jiva*) is *Brahman* limited by individual ignorance/*maya*. [see Nectar #27, "Cosmic and Individual"] *Ishvara*, the personal God, is ever aware of its identity as *Brahman* and uses *Maya* to project the universe, whereas the individual soul is under the thrall of *Maya* and bound by the consequences [i.e. desire, passions, *karma*] of being ignorant of its true nature as *Brahman*. According to *Vedanta*, the limitations of both individual ignorance and even cosmic conditioning can be transcended through spiritual disciplines, at which point, both *Ishvara*, the Cosmic Soul and the individual soul merge into *Brahman*. Thus, an essential point about the relativity of *Ishvara*, and *jiva* comes to light. Swami Vivekananda addresses this: *"Ishvara is the sum total of individuals, yet He is an Individual, as the human body is a unit, of which each cell is an individual. Samashti or collective [cosmic] equals God; Vyashti or [individual] equals the Jiva. The existence of Ishvara, therefore, depends on that of Jiva, as the body on the cell, and vice versa. Thus, Jiva and Ishvara are coexistent beings; when one exists, the other must. ...Brahman is beyond both these and is not a conditioned state; it is the only Unit not composed of many units, the principle which runs through all from a cell to God, without which nothing can exist; and whatever is real is that principle, or Brahman. When I think I am Brahman, I alone exist; so with others. Therefore, each one is the whole of that principle."* (CW, vol 5, p.269)

Some practitioners might use this teaching prematurely to reject the Personal God, the Chosen Ideal, before they are qualified for formless meditation. In his introduction to *Self-Knowledge*, Swami Nikhilananda explains in concise and lucid detail *Vedanta's* philosophy of *Brahman, Ishvara*, and the individual soul. He concludes, *"It must never be forgotten that, from the standpoint of Pure Brahman, maya is non-existent; therefore, both Ishvara and jiva are non-existent from the standpoint of the Absolute. Both are appearances. But on the relative plane, the jiva is the worshipper, and Ishvara, the worshipped. Ishvara is the Creator, and the jiva, the created being. Ishvara is the Father and Lord, and the jiva, His child or servant. Though Ishvara is one step lower than Brahman, yet His importance in the relative world is beyond all measure."* (Self-Knowledge, p. 60)

From the standpoint of practice, the question arises, which is higher? God with form or without form? Sri Krishna, in the *Bhagavad Gita*, affirms that adherents of both enter into His Being, but that meditating on the formless Imperishable *Brahman* is extremely difficult for the embodied. Thus, He assures: *"But those who worship Me, renouncing all actions in Me, regarding Me as the Supreme Goal, meditating on Me with single-minded yoga – For them whose thought is set on Me, I become very soon, the deliverer from the ocean of mortal Samsara."* (Bhagavad Gita, 12:6-7) Practicing formless meditation too soon in one's spiritual unfoldment can lead the unguided astray or slow the spiritual progress of those who are still identified with their body and unable to resist the outward movement of the mind and senses to their objects. Their minds are too restless and require something to concentrate upon. *Ishvara* is the highest form and full of divine qualities. The illumined ones and scriptures state that what we meditate upon, we become. If we meditate on the heart of a saint, we get what is in the heart of a saint, which is nothing but the Divine Being.

Sri Ramakrishna responded to this question of what is higher as follows: *"The formless aspect is of two kinds: mature and immature. The mature one is very high indeed and must be reached through God with form. The immature one...is like darkness perceived merely by closing the eyes."* (Sri Ramakrishna and His Divine Play, p. 436) He also would say with regard to peoples' temperaments and qualification, *"Some enjoy fish curry; some, fried fish; some, pickled fish; and again, some, the rich dish of fish pilau. Then too, there is difference in fitness. I ask people to learn to shoot at a banana tree first, then at the wick of a lamp, and then at a flying bird."* (Gospel, p. 910) Thus, we can conclude that great Teachers of Humanity affirm God with form is the gateway to God without form, leading to blissful dissolution into the Supreme *Brahman* who is beyond form and formlessness.

"Meditate on the Lord as thine own Self seated in your heart, who appears to you as the Universe, who is the true source of all beings. Perceive That as the primeval cause of the relationship between Consciousness and matter, and as the partless Divine Entity Transcending the three divisions of time." (Svetashvataro Upa., v. 6:5)

Within the treasure house of India's Wisdom is a teaching on four general ways that Divine Reality is known to realized beings and seekers:

Brahman – Pure Existence, Awareness, Bliss; the unaffected and unrelated Essence; Nirguna, without attributes.
Ishvara – The Personal God, the sum total of all souls; *Saguna Brahman* (with attributes)
Antaryami – The Inner Ruler Immortal, seated in the heart.
Archa – The Universal Symbol. This includes the entire universe of name and form from the earth plane to the highest heavenly realms. The existence of everything we perceive comes from the one indivisible Existence. The ancient rishis spoke of the Unchanging *Brahman* and the changing *Brahman*. Thus, objects in Nature can also be used as supports for concentration, knowing them as relative manifestations of Reality.

We can connect these in terms of form and formlessness as follows. *Brahman* and *Antaryami* are formless at 2 levels: *Brahman* (*Nirguna*) is the Supreme Formlessness, and *Antaryami* is a relative formlessness; since it is the inner guide, it is with attributes. *Ishvara*, manifests both with form and without form, but always with attributes. Since it is the sum total of all souls, it is manifesting in the individual as the *Antaryami*, the inner controller and guide. Sri Ramakrishna has summated the experience of the seeker/devotee with *Ishvara* by saying the seeker innately feels God is a person. *"It is He who listens to our prayers... It doesn't matter whether you accept God with form or not. It is enough to feel that God is a Person who listens to our prayers, who creates, preserves, and destroys the universe, and who is endowed with infinite power.* (Gospel, p. 149).

Archa, God manifesting through names and forms, is important to understand in a deep way. Swami Vivekananda, in *Bhakti Yoga*, explains the use of external and mental objects in bringing the mind to concentration. In the West, we have been raised to think of religious or spiritual images as idols and miss the point that God is being invoked through these. One of Sri Ramakrishna's Western-educated disciples complained how ignorant it was for people to worship clay images. The Master responded, *"But why clay? It is an image of Spirit."* The practitioner progresses from thinking that God is separate, "out there, somewhere," experiencing the divine presence within. When *Brahman* has been realized, the world appears as so many forms of *Brahman*. Thus, the beginner uses forms and names to call forth the presence of God to their mind, while the illumined naturally see God alone. *"All this indeed is Brahman"* is one of the conclusions of the *Upanisads*. Shankaracharya has affirmed it this way: *"It is the apt and final conclusion of the Vedanta that all is Brahman - Time, space, living beings, and the world. Living in constant realization of this is what is called Enlightenment. Brahman is one without a second, pure and perfect, And the revealed scriptures are the sure and certain proof of this fact."* (*Vivekachudamani*, v. 478)

It takes qualification to meditate on formless Reality. But it also takes qualification to meditate on anything else one chooses. That qualification is concentration. In closing, we will look briefly at how *Patanjala Yoga*, *Jnana Yoga*, and *Bhakti Yoga* (the paths of Meditation, Knowledge, and Devotion) view some of these obstacles and qualifications.

Yoga Philosophy-psychology delineates eight limbs, of which the first five need some degree of mastery before one can actually concentrate (sixth limb). These are not "rules," but observable principles. The restless mind cannot concentrate. A distracted mind is a consequence of selfish actions perpetrated due to desire for pleasure and fear of pain. *Yoga* prescribes moral practices and beneficial observances: such as nonviolence, truthfulness, non-coveting, chastity or moderation of sensual appetites, and non-greed – each of these mastered in thought, word, and deed. *Yoga* further enjoins austerity, study of scriptures, self-surrender to *Ishvara*, contentment, and purity. Only when one can withdraw the mind from objects and the thought of objects will the practitioner be able to concentrate, having eliminated all distractions. It is interesting to note that people commonly believe that meditation makes one calm, but it is really the opposite; one becomes calm by resisting the distractions of the senses and the mind's preoccupation with objects (work, wealth, relationships, the body, etc.), and then concentration and meditation can occur.

The path of Knowledge is the path of discrimination between Self and the non-Self, which one learns from the teacher and study of the revealed scriptures (being the realizations of illumined beings). Traditionally, the teachings of nonduality were not given to those without the six virtues: 1) inner peace arising from renunciation of the non-Self, 2) sense control, 3) forbearance of dualities such as heat and cold, 4) the ability to hold the mind within once it has been restrained from going out through the senses, 5) the ability to concentrate the mind on God, 6) and enthusiasm and faith in God and one's ability to realize the Truth. Finally, without a sincere longing to be liberated (know oneself as *Brahman*), unconscious desires will pull the mind away from formless meditation. Many today try to follow this path without these qualifications as if one can jump from the ground to the roof without walking up the stairs or ladder. Sri Ramakrishna cautions those who prematurely think themselves fit for nondual Truth, *"... [T]he Knowledge of Brahman is impossible without the destruction of body-consciousness. The jñāni says: 'I am Brahman; I am not the body. I am beyond hunger and thirst, disease and grief, birth and death, pleasure and pain.' How can you be a jnani if you are conscious of disease, grief, pain, pleasure, and the like?"* (Gospel, p.468)

The path of Devotion, is a path of sublimation, wherein one seeks to love God first and foremost by turning all passions, all lesser loves, toward God. One forges a relationship with the Chosen Ideal and strives to maintain it moment to moment via inner communion: as the Father or Mother, the Eternal Friend, the Master, the Divine Child, the Beloved, or the feeling of Peace. The mind achieves one-pointedness when the Chosen Ideal of God becomes its sole desire. Selfless Love and yearning concentrate the mind like nothing else. In Western culture, it seems we need a heavy dose of spiritual knowledge to ignite our Love of God so that we are loving God and not the ego. One's ability to withdraw the mind from lesser attractions is cultivated by memorizing prayers and devotional songs, by repeating the divine Name or *Mantra* of God knowing it to be identical with God, contemplating the stories and teachings associated with one's Chosen Ideal, and maintaining the company of other devoted practitioners. As Sri Ramakrishna stated earlier, by meditation on God with Form, the mature Formless Reality is attained.

Annapurna Sarada lives in Waimea, Hawaii, where she continues her studies of Vedanta with Babaji Bob Kindler, serves as the general manager of SRV Associations, and offers classes in the community and for the SRV sangha.

"I have fashioned a garland of the different religious traditions of the world, and have offered them all at the sacred Feet of the Mother of the Universe."

Sri Ramakrishna Paramahamsa

SRV Associations 2023
Dharma Visits to Portland, Oregon

Babaji Bob Kindler's Dharma Visits to Portland, OR

SRV Oregon
1922 S.E. 42nd Ave., Portland, OR 97215 | 808-990-3354 | srvinfo@srv.org

February, 2023

Feb 17	Fri	7:00pm	**Satsang** in the ashram
Feb 18	Sat	9:30am	**Class: Rudra Hrdaya Upanisad**
		6:00pm	**Sri Ramakrishna Puja**
Feb 19	Sun	9:30am	**Class: Rudra Hrdaya Upanisad**

Winter Retreat at Windwood Waters
** Four-Yoga Living **
Thursday, Feb 23rd - Monday, Feb 27th, 2023

May, 2023

May 19	Fri	7:00pm	**Satsang** in the ashram
May 20	Sat	9:30am	**Class on The Upanisads**
		6:00pm	**SRV Puja**
May 21	Sun	9:30am	**Class on The Upanisads**

Suggested Donation for classes: $20. No one turned away.

Memorial Weekend Retreat at Windwood Waters
Awakening to Mother Kundalini
Thursday, May 25th - Monday, May 29th, 2023

October, 2023

Divine Mother Retreat: The Word's Great Mother Scripture
(Srimad Devi Bhagavatam)
Thursday, October 5th - Monday, October 9th, 2023

Oct 13	Fri	7:00pm	**Satsang** in the ashram
Oct 14	Sat	9:30am	**Class on The Upanisads**
		6:00pm	**Sri Durga Puja**
Oct 15	Sun	9:30am	**Class on The Upanisads**

Suggested Donation for classes: $20. No one turned away.

Stay Informed about SRV Classes, Retreats, & Online Seminars.

Sign our email list & Explore SRV Offerings

We invite you to visit
SRV's Facebook & Instagram Pages:
Facebook.com/srvvedanta
Instagram.com/srvassociations

SRV Associations 2023
Three In-Person Retreats

For details: srvinfo@srv.org | www.srv.org

In-Person Retreats with Babaji Bob Kindler

Join us for three and a half days in the Peace-conferring atmosphere of Divine Wisdom & Devotion: classes on Divine Wisdom, its application, engaging formal and informal satsangs, & devotional music with Babaji and students.

Winter Retreat at Windwood Waters — **February 23 - 27**
Four-Yoga Living
Near Stevenson, WA

In the spirit of Swami Vivekananda's realization of the Four Yogas of Jnanam, Bhakti, Raja, and Karma as the "New Religion of this Age," deep classes of especially prepared teachings will be offered in the setting of daily meditation, and nighttime Satsang and Arati — all absorbed within the atmosphere of Sri Ramakrishna's sacred birthday puja week.

Memorial Weekend Retreat at Windwood Waters — **May 25 - 29**
Awakening to Mother Kundalini
Near Stevenson, WA

In the tradition of *Kundalini Yoga*, utilizing the textbook, *Reclaiming Kundalini Yoga*, and paying particular attention to Sri Ramakrishna's teachings and experiences with the Divine Mother, this concentrated phase of time with guru and sangha is designed to open "nadis" and conduct consciousness to deeper centers, or *chakras*, or "lotuses," that are within our subtle body. *Kundalini* does not awaken; She is ever awake. It is we who must awaken to Her.

Rare Hawaii Retreat at New Badrinath — **July 1 - 4**
We are Atman All-Abiding:
The 108 Verses on the Atman

This work on the Eternal Self has never been taken up for contemplation of its easy presentation of teachings on the Atman. With the creation of a new chart that accents them, these auspicious verses will be utilized for the purpose of inspiration and attainment along the esteemed way of the Vedanta — all in conjunction with the holy days of *Gurupurnima* and Independence Day. * NOTE: This retreat — the only one of the year in Hawaii — will only be given if there is adequate attendance, based upon interested students committing to it and sending in their retreat fees no later than June 15th.

Divine Mother Retreat — **October 5 - 9**
The World's Great Mother Scripture
Pacific Northwest, TBA

During the *Navaratri* season in October, which falls over Columbus Day weekend, the incomparable wisdom of Sri Durga and Her various Goddess forms will be transmitted in retreat by consulting and studying the world's greatest Divine Mother scripture, *The Srimad Devi Bhagavatam*. The guru's long-standing study and communion with this powerful scripture will afford students the opportunity to imbibe rare expressions of Indian Dharma and Nonduality – straight from the Source, Herself.

SRV Associations 2023
Online Weekend Seminars with Babaji Bob Kindler

Two full days of classes on the Wisdom of Mother India & engaging satsangs with Babaji and students.

Seminar 1
From Ram, To Krishna, To Sri Ramakrishna   April 1 & 2
Vedanta-based Teachings of the Avatar

To know about the Avatar is to discover that He does not come only once, nor come many times as separate individuals, but that He is ever-one and comes many times over several yugas. The proof of this is in His teachings over ages, which reconfirm certain eternal and irrefutable principles that are central to India's Vedanta. In this engaging seminar, these axioms will be accented and contemplated in an atmosphere conducive to their realization — for all times.

Seminar 2
Insights & Impediments while Following the Spiritual Path   June 24 & 25

Surfacing karmas | Unpredictable changing of the three gunas over cycles of time | The oft-times weighty influence of the hidden ancestor realm | A confusing upbringing amongst anti-religious or fundamentalist families, relatives, and siblings | The continual pressure from present day society and its selfish and violent ways — Amidst all these and more, serious seekers of God and Truth must attempt to find, follow, and finalize the definitive journey to the Source of Existence. Insights can help or hinder; impediments can do the same. This seminar will clarify many such distinctions, leaving the aspirant in possession of effective weapons with which to offset and even dispel all the obstacles listed here.

Seminar 3
The West's Heaven & Hell, The East's Nirvana and & Samsara;   August 12 & 13
Christianity's Sin and Salvation, India's Karma and Liberation

Much of what is now beneficial in our lives, and all that is still detrimental, can be generally attributed to the presence of dharma in our upbringing or the lack thereof. Being raised with deluded religious precepts, called *Bhrantidarshana*/false seeing, by the father of Yoga, leaves individuals, families, even whole nations, in philosophical quandary and religious confusion in the end, i.e., at the end of a lifetime. This unfortunate fate and the suffering it causes is unnecessary, bringing to mind the expression, "a huge waste of time." Using Swami Aseshanandaji's teachings, this seminar will expose and juxtapose the untenable philosophical propositions which many of us were raised with in contrast to the Nondual Truth of India's Sanatana Dharma — both of which this Hindu-born, Christian college trained, monastic swami and sannyasin of India, had deep insight into and extensive experience with. Excerpts from Babaji's new book in progress, "Advaita Vedanta in a Jivanmukta," will be shared, along with ten newer teachings charts.

Seminar 4
Crystal Clarity and Cosmic Subterfuge   September 23 & 24
Brahman, Shakti, Atman, Prakriti, and Maya

Beyond the narrow "one world, one body, one lifetime" perspective of today's Western religion and philosophy, which has convinced most of earthly humanity that matter is the only reality, there is the much deeper view of India's revelation of seven worlds and three bodies — all propounded in order to lead souls to liberation in the "Great Spirit." That "Spirit" is Consciousness, or pure, original Awareness according to Mother India. It is declared to be nondual and indivisible by those who have experienced It, but undoubtedly It has Its sport; or put another way, there is sportive play, or *Lila*, in It. Just as a vast, homogenous body of water called an ocean sometimes gives rise to multiple waves breaking across its surface, so too does this Sentient Sea of Awareness produce activity and motion on Its blissfull breast. This Essence and Its enigmas will be explored in this seminar, offering up insights for deep contemplation and meditation.

Seminar 5
The Matri Avatar Teachings of Sri Sarada Devi   December 9 & 10

In advance of another of Babaji's forthcoming books, entitled *"Teachings of the Matri Avatar: A Holy Mother Mandala,"* this seminar will plunge deep into our *Paramaguru's* disarmingly straightforward teaching transmission capable of and designed for stripping off the unwanted encrustations of mayic life in the present and ongoing Kali Yuga. Fifteen new charts sporting various beautiful mandalas, and images of the Holy Mother throughout Her previous lifetime — each petal filled with the sacred words She offered us — will be viewed and studied over the two-day course of this "must see, must hear, must be there" seminar.

 Learn More at srvinfo@srv.org | www.srv.org>retreats

Raja Yoga Correspondence Course

An in-depth study of Patanjali's Yoga Sutras with Babaji Bob Kindler.

Contact: srvinfo@srv.org

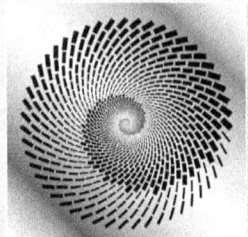

This meditative state is the highest state of existence. So long as there is desire, no real happiness can come.

It is only the contemplative, witness-like study of objects that brings to us real enjoyment and happiness. It is only to the soul that has attained to this contemplative state that the world really becomes beautiful.

To him who desires nothing, and does not mix himself up with them, the manifold changes of nature are one panorama of beauty and sublimity.

— Swami Vivekananda

A Ground-Breaking Interfaith Program

In the Spirit Interviews with Lex Hixon

From the early 1970's through the late 1980's, Lex Hixon hosted **In the Spirit** from WBAI, in NYC. As a list, the fruit of this selfless work reads like a comprehensive Who's Who of the spiritual, artistic and intellectual heart and mind of both Eastern and Western cultures. Over 300 programs can be downloaded at www.srv.org

- Kalu Rinpoche
- Sakya Trizin
- Dudjom Rinpoche
- Tartan Tulku
- Trungpa Rinpoche
- Bernie Glassman
- Master Shen Yen
- Rebbi Gedalia
- Rabbi Zalman Schachter
- Rabbi Dovid Din
- Sheikh Muzafer
- Guru Bawa
- Pir Vilayet Khan
- Swami Muktananda
- Meher Baba
- Sri Chinmoy
- Ram Das
- Swami Rama
- Mother Teresa
- Father Daniel Barrigan
- Programs on Meister Eckhart, Padre Pio, Mother Mary, Jesus Christ
- Programs on Sri Ramakrishna, Divine Mother, Ramana Maharishi, Sri Aurobindo

Hearing about Brahman is good.

Taking teachings on Brahman is better.

Meditating directly on Brahman is better still.

But best of all is that meditation in which all doubt about the nature of Reality dies away forever.

—Shankaracharya's *Crest Jewel of Discrimination*

Dharma Weekends at SRV Associations

Online & in-person with
Babaji Bob Kindler, Spiritual Director

Satsang
Join us for Q & A
Bring your questions from classes and studies

Saturdays at 8:00am HST
On Zoom

Brahman Bytes
Group Philosophical Discussion

Saturdays at 10:00am HST
On Zoom from community.srvwisdom.org

Sunday Class
Vedanta, Yoga, Tantra

Sundays at 2:30pm HST
On Zoom & in person

Schedule Subject to Change | Sign up for schedule emails: srv.org

Dharma Art Wisdom Charts
www.dharmaartwisdomcharts.com

SRV Websites:
www.srv.org
community.SRVWisdom.org
www.nectarofnondualtruth.org

Order Dharma Charts for your:

Meditation Room • Yoga Studio
Temple • Classroom • Home • Office

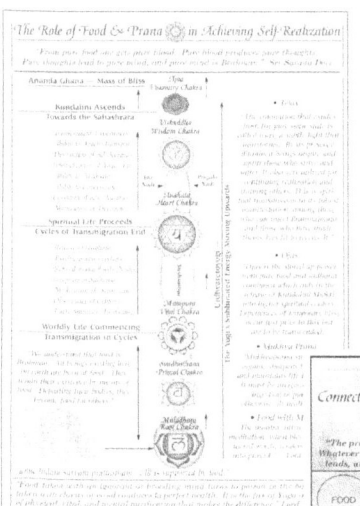

Bring the Light of Wisdom into Conversations.

Discuss Dharma with your Children, Friends, Co-Workers, Relatives, & Students

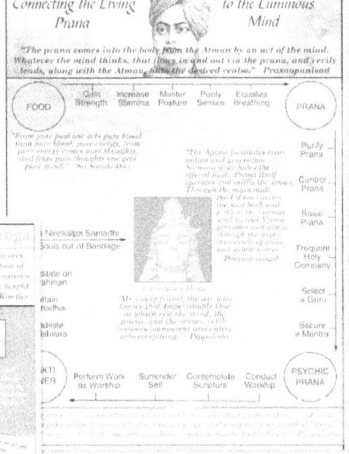

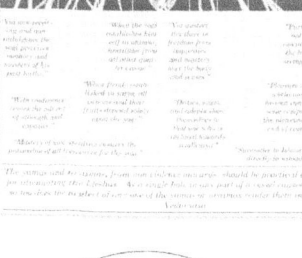

Archival Ink
Full Size: 2' x 3'
Ready to frame

Explore Mother India's Timeless Wisdom

www.srv.org
- Sanskrit Chants to Learn & Practice
- "In the Spirit" Audio Interviews
- Teachings for Youth/Children
- Articles on SRV Ideals, Teachers, & Wisdom
- Sacred Books & Music online store
- This website is the hub for everything SRV....

Join the Ashram of the Subtle Realms:

community.SRVWisdom.org
- Spiritual Community
- Easy access to: live classes, archived video and audio classes
- Nectar of Non-Dual Truth back issues
- Special discounts for books, charts, and a retreat of your choice.

Nectar of Non-Dual Truth—A Journal of Universal Religious & Philosophical Teachings

www.nectarofnondualtruth.org
- Learn about Nectar's mission
- Preview upcoming articles and writers
- Order back issues

Dharma Art Wisdom Charts—For the Study of Wisdom

Dharmaartwisdomcharts.com
- Beautiful, essential Wisdom charts for Home, School, Spiritual Center, and Yoga Studios.
- Archival inks, ready to frame

YouTube Channel Class Series with Babaji Bob Kindler

Youtube.com/user/SRVAssociations
- Mother's Path of Nonduality
- God/Brahman Reflected in the Universe
- Non-Touch Yoga of Gaudapada
- The Third Eye & Kundalini's 7 Chakras
- Spiritual Interviews
- Satsangs, Sacred Music Videos, & more

Comments about Nectar from our Readers

"For a long time there was a crying need for such a journal to spread the message of Neo-Vedanta especially in the West. We hope this one will fill the void. We have gone through it and were enchanted by its contents and presentation...."

Swami Videhatmananda,
Editor, Vivek Jyoti

"Nectar's tenets are refreshing and uplifting such as, 'This is one of the aims of our SRV journal, to show that all practice along the spiritual path can and should be undertaken with the fore-knowledge of our essential oneness with God.' [It is rare] for a spiritual entity to express 'true' friendship with other spiritual entities and religions...."

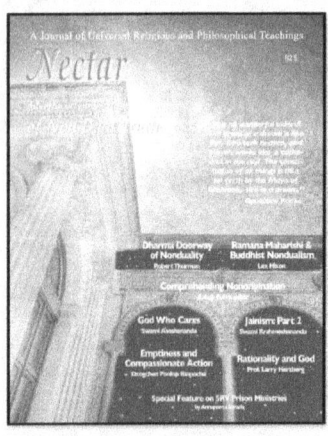

"I very much appreciate your detailed presentation of Advaita Vedanta, Sri Ramakrishna, and Mother Kali. I hope it will reach a large number of American Citizens."

President Maharaj,
Ramakrishna Order
Swami Ranganathananda

"I'm dazzled by a tradition that truly acknowledges the deepest held truths held by different religions and I know that this is a rare thing. I am delighted to find the pearls of wisdom shared in this journal from other traditions such as Judaism, Sufism, Buddhism, Hinduism, Vedanta, Islam, etc., acknowledged and held high along with the truths of SRV's Tradition."

Sacred Music from Hawaii

Jai Ma Music
The Music of Babaji Bob Kindler

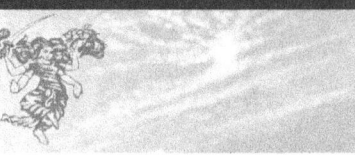

Chanting • Instrumental • Devotional • Poetry

Kali Bol Ramakrishna
Gita Govinda Mala
Hari Om Ramanam
Guru Bhajans
Jai Ho Vivekananda!
Siva! Siva!
Hymns to the Goddess
Shakti Bhajans
Deva Devi Svarupaya
Kali Bol
Sarada Ramakrishna Name
Hymns to the Master & Mother
108 Names of Sarada
Universal Aspects
Bhajananda
Avatar Bhajans
Puja/Arati Hymns
Wingspan
Music from the Matrix I
Music from the Matrix II
Waters of Life
Ever Free Never Bound
Tiger's Paw
Sound Castles
Worlds Unseen
Ecstatic Songs of Ramprasad I
Ecstatic Songs of Ramprasad II

Available at www.SRV.org
And your favorite streaming service.

Advaita-satya-amritam

Of Non-Dual Truth

Subscription Form

Order Next Issue by March 1 2024

Annual Subscription: $18 (U.S.)
Annual Subscription: $25 (International)
Nectar is mailed out once each year in the Spring

Subscribe online: www.srv.org > Nectar Journal > Subscribe
Scan this QR code and you will be right there!

Or, Subscribe by check:
Please fill out the back side of this form and mail it with your check to:
SRV Associations, PO Box 1364, Honokaa, HI 96727 (*payable to: SRV Associations*)
MasterCard or Visa accepted via phone as well:
808-990-3354 • srvinfo@srv.org • www.srv.org

#38

Advaita-satya-amritam

Of Non-Dual Truth

Subscription Form

Order Next Issue by March 1 2024

Annual Subscription: $18 (U.S.)
Annual Subscription: $25 (International)
Nectar is mailed out once each year in the Spring

Subscribe online: www.srv.org > Nectar Journal > Subscribe
Scan this QR code and you will be right there!

Or, Subscribe by check:
Please fill out the back side of this form and mail it with your check to:
SRV Associations, PO Box 1364, Honokaa, HI 96727 (*payable to: SRV Associations*)
MasterCard or Visa accepted via phone as well:
808-990-3354 • srvinfo@srv.org • www.srv.org

#38

Advaita-satya-amritam

NECTAR

Of Non-Dual Truth

Subscription Form

Order Next Issue by March 1 2024

Annual Subscription: $18 (U.S.)
Annual Subscription: $25 (International)
Nectar is mailed out once each year in the Spring

Subscribe online: www.srv.org > Nectar Journal > Subscribe
Scan this QR code and you will be right there!

Or, Subscribe by check:
Please fill out the back side of this form and mail it with your check to:
SRV Associations, PO Box 1364, Honokaa, HI 96727 (*payable to: SRV Associations*)
MasterCard or Visa accepted via phone as well:
808-990-3354 • srvinfo@srv.org • www.srv.org

#38

Your Shipping information: (if subscribing by mail)

Name: _____

Address: _____

City, State, Zip: _____

Email: _____

You Can Help Others Receive Nectar.   Your gift is tax-deductible.

We continue to supply free copies to prison inmates, religious organizations, and persons requiring financial assistance. You can help bridge the financial gap with a separate donation to Nectar. You will receive both our sincere gratitude and a donation letter for your taxes. SRV Associations is a 501c3 tax exempt religious organization.

MasterCard or Visa accepted online at www.srv.org > Giving
Or you can pay by credit card over the phone.
808-990-3354 • srvinfo@srv.org • www.srv.org • Questions? Call or write us!

Your Shipping information: (if subscribing by mail)

Name: _____

Address: _____

City, State, Zip: _____

Email: _____

You Can Help Others Receive Nectar.   Your gift is tax-deductible.

We continue to supply free copies to prison inmates, religious organizations, and persons requiring financial assistance. You can help bridge the financial gap with a separate donation to Nectar. You will receive both our sincere gratitude and a donation letter for your taxes. SRV Associations is a 501c3 tax exempt religious organization.

MasterCard or Visa accepted online at www.srv.org > Giving
Or you can pay by credit card over the phone.
808-990-3354 • srvinfo@srv.org • www.srv.org • Questions? Call or write us!

Your Shipping information: (if subscribing by mail)

Name: _____

Address: _____

City, State, Zip: _____

Email: _____

You Can Help Others Receive Nectar.   Your gift is tax-deductible.

We continue to supply free copies to prison inmates, religious organizations, and persons requiring financial assistance. You can help bridge the financial gap with a separate donation to Nectar. You will receive both our sincere gratitude and a donation letter for your taxes. SRV Associations is a 501c3 tax exempt religious organization.

MasterCard or Visa accepted online at www.srv.org > Giving
Or you can pay by credit card over the phone.
808-990-3354 • srvinfo@srv.org • www.srv.org • Questions? Call or write us!

www.ingramcontent.com/pod-product-compliance
Lightning Source LLC
Chambersburg PA
CBHW081630100526
44590CB00021B/3675